ML

D1569668

Social Issues
in Literature

War in
Ernest Hemingway's
A Farewell to Arms

Other Books in the Social Issues in Literature Series:

Social Issues
in Literature

War in
Ernest Hemingway's
A Farewell to Arms

David Haugen and Susan Musser, Book Editors

GREENHAVEN PRESS
A part of Gale, Cengage Learning

GALE
CENGAGE Learning·

Farmington Hills, Mich • San Francisco • New York • Waterville, Maine
Meriden, Conn • Mason, Ohio • Chicago

GALE
CENGAGE Learning·

Elizabeth Des Chenes, *Director, Content Strategy*
Cynthia Sanner, *Publisher*
Douglas Dentino, *Manager, New Product*

© 2014 Greenhaven Press, a part of Gale, Cengage Learning

WCN: 01 100 101

Gale and Greenhaven Press are registered trademarks used herein under license.

For more information, contact:
Greenhaven Press
27500 Drake Rd.
Farmington Hills, MI 48331-3535
Or you can visit our Internet site at gale.cengage.com

For product information and technology assistance, contact us at

Gale Customer Support, 1-800-877-4253
For permission to use material from this text or product, submit all requests online at www.cengage.com/permissions

Further permissions questions can be emailed to permissionrequest@cengage.com

Articles in Greenhaven Press anthologies are often edited for length to meet page requirements. In addition, original titles of these works are changed to clearly present the main thesis and to explicitly indicate the author's opinion. Every effort is made to ensure that Greenhaven Press accurately reflects the original intent of the authors. Every effort has been made to trace the owners of copyrighted material.

Cover image © Everett Collection Inc./Alamy.

LIBRARY OF CONGRESS CATALOGING-IN-PUBLICATION DATA

War in Ernest Hemingway's A farewell to arms / David Haugen and Susan Musser, book editors.
    pages cm. -- (Social Issues in Literature)
    Includes bibliographical references and index.
    ISBN 978-0-7377-6395-9 (hardcover) -- ISBN 978-0-7377-6396-6 (pbk.)
    1. Hemingway, Ernest, 1899-1961. Farewell to arms. 2. Hemingway, Ernest, 1899-1961--Study and teaching. 3. World War, 1914-1918--United States--Literature and the war. 4. War in literature. 5. War--Psychological aspects--Study and teaching. 6. War and society--Study and teaching. I. Haugen, David M., 1969- editor of compilation. II. Musser, Susan, editor of compilation.
    PS3515.E37F359 2014
    813'.52--dc23
                                                                    2013036416

Printed in Mexico
1 2 3 4 5 6 7 18 17 16 15 14

Contents

Chapter 1: Background on Ernest Hemingway

Ira Elliott

Ernest Hemingway's spare, forthright writing style and his uncompromising, uncomplaining heroes are hallmarks of his novels and short stories. Many critics and readers also assume these traits reflect the author's stoic attitude and masculine lifestyle. Regardless of whether his own story can be read into his fiction, both Hemingway's life experiences and his prose style have left an indelible mark on modern literature.

A Farewell to Arms
Robert W. Lewis

Although Hemingway was pleased with his depiction of war as he knew it to be, reception of *A Farewell to Arms* was mixed. Hemingway's defenders found the work to be a frank and just portrayal as well as an exemplar of modernist style, but some critics derided the book as too vulgar for readers or riddled with overblown emotions that seemed disproportionate to the subject matter.

Chapter 2: War in *A Farewell to Arms*

and Masculinity
Lawrence R. Broer

A Farewell to Arms depicts violence and war with realistic detail that makes it difficult to celebrate. However, the novel still presents soldiers as glorious in battle, and it offers a protagonist who is insensitive to the violence occurring around him, who commits acts of violence without evident remorse, and who admires masculine behavior.

The narrative of *A Farewell to Arms* is Frederic Henry's retelling of his wartime experiences and the tragedies and losses he faced. However, his attempt to find closure and healing through the process of narrative is continually ruptured by the pain of those past memories—a pain that he will endure in the present every time he tries to find meaning in the trauma of those life-changing events.

A Farewell to Arms examines the worth of four types of ideals—service to God, service to one's country, service to a person one loves, and service to the sick and wounded. Ultimately, the novel rejects all these in favor of a personal conviction based on bravery and stoicism, which Hemingway presents as the only religion that affords one a sense of immortality in the face of death.

Chapter 3: Contemporary Perspectives on War

Historically, wars were first fought in the name of God and then in the name of one's king; then for love of country became the new motivation for which people fought. However, in the modern world, it is not enough to go to war to protect the honor of one's country. Instead, militaries are called upon to serve the security of the global community, and this peacekeeping intention must be stressed to ensure that war is justified.

American acceptance of war and the deaths that sometimes accompany military service is closely tied to the widespread belief in the Christian ideal of sacrifice that reveres individuals for giving of themselves to protect freedom and other national ideals.

Introduction

L ate in Ernest Hemingway's novel *A Farewell to Arms*, American ambulance driver Frederic Henry decides to desert from his duties with the Italian army during World War I and abandon the soldiering life. Stripping himself of his shirt and the insignia that mark him as an officer, he rides a troop train away from the front, wishing only that he might once again see his beloved Catherine, the nurse who helped him recover from a battlefield wound months earlier and who has since become his lover. Frederic waits for the train ride to end, knowing that he will walk away from the military for good. He holds a newspaper but refuses to read it, stating, "I did not want to read about the war. I was going to forget the war. I had made a separate peace." Forgetting the war, for Frederic, though, is not an easy task. While his desire for Catherine persists in his waking dreams on that train ride, Frederic's thoughts also turn to the comrades he will leave behind. Frederic may claim he has made a separate peace, but he and the reader know the war has left indelible scars on his mind and body.

Critics differ in their opinions about whether to categorize *A Farewell to Arms* as a war novel or a romance. Regardless of how one approaches the novel, the presence of the war and its effects on Frederic Henry are major factors that shape the narrative. Published in 1929, the work evidently draws on Hemingway's own service as an ambulance driver in the war that was then only a decade in the past. Like Frederic's resolve to find a separate peace, Hemingway may have titled his novel to suggest his own peace with that conflict and perhaps a hope that the world had learned from the futility of "the war to end all wars." However, in the preface to the 1949 edition, the author notes, "The title of this book is *A Farewell to Arms* and except for three years there has been war of some kind almost ever since it has been written." Hemingway knew first-hand the horrors of war, and he condemned the pursuit of war as an evil crime perpetrated by those who stood to profit from the bloodshed. At the same time, Hemingway believed that combat gave soldiers an opportunity to face death with a stalwart determination that signaled a mastery of the fear of mortality. He had a certain fondness for this grim heroism, showing clearly in *A Farewell to Arms* how it created a unique bond between soldiers. In the 1949 preface, Hemingway extols, "Wars are fought by the finest people that there are, or just say people, although, the closer you are to where they are fighting, the finer people you meet." The "finer people"—the ones who must live with the ever presence of death—are noble in comparison to the "swine" he subsequently mentions who provoke warfare for their own gain.

War, however, to Hemingway, does not simply create selfless heroes among the rank and file. Frederic Henry sees nothing glorious or honorable about war; he finds such terms "obscene." In a letter he penned while writing *For Whom the Bell Tolls*, his novel about the Spanish Civil War, Hemingway attested, "I would like to be able to write understandingly about both deserters and heroes, cowards and brave men, traitors and men who are not capable of being traitors." Referring to his own experience as a reporter during that conflict, he concluded, "We learned a lot about all such people." Frederic Henry is both a hero and deserter. He has seen the realities of war, and he chooses to flee as the justifications for such senseless murder begin to unravel and the capriciousness of fate becomes apparent. As critic Michael John MacDonald IV states in the fall 2008 issue of the British periodical the *Explicator*, "The resonating theme of *A Farewell to Arms* echoes Hemingway's disdain for the abstract notions of faith and honor that contrast with the concrete facts of war. As Frederic comes to terms with the meaninglessness of abstract ideas, such as duty and conscience towards one's office, he must deal with the futility of life." Frederic wants something to believe in, but the rhetoric of bravery and glory offer only illusions. His response is to seek love with Catherine and turn forever from war.

What Frederic simultaneously recognizes and avoids, though, is the unsettling truth that the solace he desires in the love of Catherine is also an illusion fostered, in part, by the nightmarish circumstances of war. Catherine has lost her fiancé to the war, and she has also cast off any pretenses concerning the honor of a battlefield death. At one point in their intimate relationship, Catherine has Frederic stand in for her dead fiancé and asks him to say that he has "come back" to her, invoking the spirit of her lost love. She even refers to their romance as "a rotten game we play," revealing a world-weary cynicism that does not bode well for the idyllic love in which Frederic wants to believe. Like Frederic, Catherine carries scars—wounds inflicted by the trauma of war and its absurdities, and it is clear that such scars would never heal, no matter how long the pair continued to play their game.

Perhaps it is the presence of these wounds that, as some reviewers have stipulated, make the title of Hemingway's novel ironic. Indeed, as the author admitted, the title can only be—intentionally or not—read ironically in a real-world context, given that human beings did not bid farewell to warfare at the end of "the war to end all wars." This is not to say, however, that Hemingway's commentaries on brutality, nationalism, life, and love have lost their critical edge. As the essays in *Social Issues in Literature: War in Ernest Hemingway's "A Farewell to Arms"* exemplify, the novel still provokes readers to interpret Hemingway's words and define his stance. Some reviewers argue that the war is simply a backdrop for the romance between Frederic and Catherine; others believe that it is a traumatizing force that scars the narrative. This anthology offers several approaches to understanding the relevance of war and death in *A Farewell to Arms* to the author, to the characters, and to the reader.

Chronology

July 21, 1899
Ernest Miller Hemingway is born to Clarence Edmonds Hemingway and Grace Hall Hemingway in the Chicago suburb of Oak Park, Illinois.

January 1916
Hemingway's first piece of published writing appears in his high school newspaper.

October 1917
After graduating from high school, Hemingway begins reporting for the *Kansas City Star*. He also enlists with the Missouri National Guard as a member of the 7th Missouri Infantry.

May 1918
Hemingway travels to Italy to serve as an ambulance driver for the American Red Cross during World War I.

July 8, 1918
After a trip to the canteen to gather supplies to deliver to soldiers on the front line, Hemingway is injured by mortar fire but still carries an Italian soldier out of danger. He is awarded the Italian Silver Medal of Bravery for his actions. During his stay at the hospital, he meets and falls in love with a Red Cross nurse, Agnes von Kurowsky. These incidents are often cited as the basis for *A Farewell to Arms*.

1920
Hemingway begins writing articles for the *Toronto Star* after being discharged from the Red Cross the previous year.

September 3, 1921
Hemingway marries Hadley Richardson. After two months, Hemingway begins working as the foreign correspondent for the *Toronto Star*, and the newlyweds move to Paris.

October 10, 1923

Hemingway's first son, John Hadley Nicanor Hemingway, is born in Toronto.

1923

Three Stories and Ten Poems, a collection of short stories and poems, is published in Paris. It is Hemingway's first published work.

1925

Hemingway meets F. Scott Fitzgerald the same year in which *The Great Gatsby* is published. The work inspires Hemingway to write a novel, and he begins work on what will become *The Sun Also Rises*.

1926

Scribner's offers the author a contract, and the publishing house releases *The Sun Also Rises* in October.

1927

Hemingway and his wife divorce in January, and he marries Pauline Pfeiffer in May. *Men Without Women* is published in October.

1928

Hemingway and his new wife move back to the United States and settle in Key West, Florida, in March. On June 28, their son Patrick is born after a difficult delivery. This again is seen as a reference point for *A Farewell to Arms*. Later in the fall, Hemingway learns that his father has committed suicide.

1929

A Farewell to Arms is published by Scribner's. While in Spain, Hemingway begins to research his next book, *Death in the Afternoon*, a nonfiction book about bullfighting.

November 12, 1931
Pauline gives birth to the author's third son, Gregory Hancock Hemingway.

1932
Death in the Afternoon is published.

1933
During a ten-week trip to Africa, Hemingway begins collecting material for the nonfiction book *Green Hills of Africa* and other short stories. The short story collection *Winner Take Nothing* is also published this year.

1935
Green Hills of Africa receives mixed reviews upon publication.

1937
The author's only novel of the 1930s, *To Have and Have Not*, is published. *Time* magazine runs his picture on the front cover.

March 1937
In the wake of the start of the Spanish Civil War, Hemingway begins working as a war correspondent for the North American Newspaper Alliance (NANA).

1938
The Fifth Column and the First Forty-Nine Stories is published by Scribner's.

1940
The Broadway production of *The Fifth Column*, Hemingway's only full-length play, opens. Hemingway and Pauline divorce, and he marries Martha Gellhorn on November 20. The couple makes Ketchum, Idaho, their summer residence and spends winters in Cuba. Scribner's publishes *For Whom the Bell Tolls* in October. The work earns Hemingway a Pulitzer Prize nomination.

1941

Hemingway accompanies Martha on an assignment to China for the magazine *Collier's*, and he sends articles to the newspaper *PM*. The couple sees the effects of the war between China and Japan.

June to December 1944

Hemingway works as a war correspondent throughout Europe during World War II.

1945

Martha Gellhorn and Hemingway divorce.

1946

Hemingway marries Mary Welsh.

1947

Hemingway is awarded the Bronze Star for bravery during World War II.

1950

Across the River and Into the Trees, a novel based on a love affair between Hemingway and 19-year-old Adriana Ivancich in Venice, garners negative reviews upon publication.

1952

The Old Man and the Sea is published.

1953

Hemingway is awarded the Pulitzer Prize for *The Old Man and the Sea*.

1954

While on a trip to Africa, Hemingway and Mary live through two separate plane crashes. The ordeals leave the author severely injured. In October, Hemingway wins the Nobel Prize in Literature.

1957
After battling illness and pain, Hemingway begins work on *A Moveable Feast* after returning to Cuba from a European trip.

1959
Life pays Hemingway to travel to Spain to write an article series on bullfighting.

July 2, 1961
Hemingway commits suicide at his home in Ketchum, Idaho, by shooting himself with a shotgun.

1964
A Moveable Feast is published posthumously.

1970
Islands in the Stream is published.

1972
A compilation of short stories entitled *The Nick Adams Stories* is published.

1985
The Dangerous Summer is published.

1986
The Garden of Eden is published.

1999
True at First Light is published one hundred years after Hemingway's birth. Scholars and critics debate whether and how authors' works should be published following their death.

Social Issues
in Literature

CHAPTER 1

Background on
Ernest Hemingway

Ernest Hemingway's Life and Works

Ira Elliott

Ira Elliott is a literary scholar who has often written about Ernest Hemingway.

Between the 1920s and 1950s, American author Ernest Hemingway wrote a series of novels and short stories that dealt with war, love, and loss in a fresh, uncompromising style that earned him lasting literary respect and public popularity. In the following viewpoint, Ira Elliott traces Hemingway's writing career, emphasizing how the attitudes and experiences of his bold and unflinching male heroes seemed to mirror the escapades and lifestyle of the author. For example, it was Hemingway's own service as a Red Cross ambulance driver in World War I that colored the outlook of the fictional ambulance driver Frederic Henry in A Farewell to Arms. *Elliott affirms that it is Hemingway's spare, direct style and adventurous and frank subject matter that have ensured the author's continuing influence on twentieth-century literature and popular culture at large.*

Ernest Hemingway was born to Dr. Clarence E. Hemingway and Grace Hall Hemingway on 21 July 1899 in Oak Park, Illinois, a Chicago suburb. He died of a self-inflicted gunshot wound on 2 July 1961 in Ketchum, Idaho, a small town outside of Sun Valley, the famous ski resort. Word of his death made front-page news around the world.

At the time of his death, Hemingway was one of the most famous men in the world and one of the foremost writers of his time. In his sixty-two years, he had lived in or traveled ex-

Ira Elliott, "Ernest Hemingway," *Writers for Young Adults*, vol. 3, Ted Hipple, ed. MI: Cengage, 1997. From Hipple. *Writers for Young Adults*, 1E. © 1997 Gale, a part of Cengage Learning, Inc. Reproduced by permission.

tensively throughout the United States, Europe, and Africa. He had witnessed or participated in World Wars I and II, the Spanish Civil War, the Greco-Turkish War, and the Sino-Japanese War. He was known worldwide as a big-game hunter, a deep-sea fisherman, a bullfight aficionado (enthusiast), and an all-around sportsman and athlete. He had been married four times and had fathered three sons.

Writer, Sportsman, Celebrity

Most of Hemingway's novels, and several of his short stories, have been made into feature films. He has inspired several full-length biographies, scores of personal remembrances by family and friends, and many books of criticism. During his life, Hemingway was a public figure whose every move was reported in the newspapers and magazines of his day. Even more than thirty years after his death, he remains a powerful presence in the world. It is difficult to think of the Spanish bullfight or the African safari without also thinking of Hemingway. Writing awards and contests bear his name. His own former high school in Oak Park has been renamed Ernest Hemingway High. Monuments erected in his honor stand in Spain, Cuba, and the United States. He sometimes appears as a character in books and films. And Hemingway's former homes in Key West, Florida, and San Francisco de Paula, Cuba, are now museums dedicated to his memory.

But if not for the writing itself, none of this fame and notoriety would matter. Hemingway's phrases have enriched our language. You will often hear references to "grace under pressure," "a moveable feast," "to have and have not," "winner take nothing," "the snows of Kilimanjaro," "death in the afternoon," or "a clean well-lighted place," all phrases coined or popularized by Hemingway. And scenes in his fiction live in the mind long after you stop reading: the bullfight fiesta in Pamplona, Spain; lion hunting in Africa; duck shooting near Venice, Italy; fishing in Michigan; wartime battles in Italy and Spain.

Ernest Hemingway peruses a page of his writing from a typewriter at his desk. © Hulton-Deutsch Collection/Corbis.

The Hemingway Hero

When Hemingway won the Nobel Prize in Literature in 1954, the Nobel Foundation said that he had "created a new style in modern literature." This new style was plain and simple. It employed everyday language and realistic dialogue. It marked a break with the "literary" language that many nineteenth-century writers had used. His style set the pattern for generations of authors and spawned countless imitators.

Hemingway's subject matter was also new and bold. He wrote frankly about love, war, and death. He believed that a person's true character came out in the face of a violent death, when you can tell if a person is courageous or cowardly, strong or weak, honest or dishonest. This is one reason that he wrote often about war and bullfighting.

Hemingway created what is often called the Hemingway hero or the code hero: a man who faces danger head-on, who looks at the harsh realities of life without blinking, and who never cracks or complains. No matter how tough things get, the Hemingway hero always exhibits "grace under pressure." This figure defined for a generation of men what it means to be a man and how manhood was achieved. On the other hand, many readers find Hemingway's female characters unreal and claim that his work puts down women. Yet in the 1980s and 1990s, Hemingway scholars have been taking another look at this element of his work. Many of these scholars have concluded that his attitude toward men and women both is far more complicated than we used to think. His work has much to say about male and female roles in society.

A central theme in Hemingway's work is how the individual fits into society, and how one should live in what often seems to be a crazy and difficult world. This issue is explored in many of Hemingway's early short stories that focus on Nick Adams, Hemingway's young alter ego. Some stories portray Nick as a child, others as a teenager in love, and still others as a young man in war. They show Nick struggling to find his own identity and his place in the world. They are stories that nearly everyone can relate to, for everyone must answer the same questions: Who am I? Where do I fit in?

From Novice Reporter to
War Correspondent

Hemingway began to write in high school for the student newspaper. Immediately after graduation in 1917, he joined the *Kansas City Star* as a junior reporter. Like most newspapers, the *Star* had what is called a stylebook, which provides reporters with advice on how to write. At the *Star*, Hemingway learned to write short, clear sentences. He would later call this the "true simple declarative sentence" in *A Moveable Feast* (1964). In *Death in the Afternoon* (1932), his nonfiction book on the Spanish bullfight, Hemingway wrote about his own "greatest difficulty" as a young writer. The problem, he said, was to find "the sequence of motion and fact which made the emotion." He meant that a good writer has to be honest with himself or herself. The good writer must understand his or her own feelings and what led to those feelings. Then, and only then, can the reader experience the same emotion.

Hemingway did not stay in Kansas City for long. War had broken out in Europe and he wanted to be where the action was. A bad eye kept him out of the armed forces, and so he signed up with the Red Cross as an ambulance driver. He was subsequently wounded in Italy while rescuing a comrade, received medals from the Italian and U.S. governments, and returned to Oak Park in 1919. He soon found work at the *Toronto Star* and with his first wife, Hadley Richardson, got just what he had hoped for: passage to Paris in 1920 as a European correspondent for the paper.

In Paris, Hemingway met other American writers, whom Gertrude Stein called members of the lost generation. This was the generation that had gone through World War I. The war had brought about so many changes in society that they were "lost" in a topsy-turvy world, what the poet T.S. Eliot called a "waste land." The question for these men and women was, how does one live in a world without stability, without security? Hemingway's answer was the code hero: men and women must be true to their own values, their personal code.

Novels of Love and War

The Sun Also Rises, Hemingway's first full-length novel, appeared in 1926 and confirmed the promise of his earlier short story collection, *In Our Time* (1925). *The Sun Also Rises* is now widely regarded as one of the most important works of twentieth-century literature. The novel tells the story of Jake Barnes, an American journalist wounded in World War I, and the woman he loves but cannot marry, Lady Brett Ashley. In the novel, Hemingway depicts the chaos of postwar Europe and deals openly with sex, a largely forbidden subject before he and other "lost generation" writers first explored it. *The Sun Also Rises* fixed the characters of Jake and Brett in the public mind. After its publication, young men and women on college campuses modeled their speech, actions, and attire on the characters in the novel.

Hemingway's second collection of stories, *Men Without Women*, was published in 1927, the year that he divorced his first wife in order to marry Pauline Pfeiffer. This was also the year in which his father committed suicide. In 1928, the Hemingways purchased a large house in Key West, where his second and third sons were born. This is also where he completed the work on his second novel, *A Farewell to Arms*.

Published in 1929, *A Farewell to Arms* tells the story of the doomed romance between an American ambulance driver and an English nurse. Hemingway's novel is regarded as one of the major works to have come out of the war, and as one of Hemingway's best. The teenage ambulance driver, Frederic Henry, narrates the story. When he falls in love with Catherine Barkley, the war keeps them apart. They soon reject the war, however, and they also reject society. They make "a separate peace" for themselves and escape the war in Italy and Switzerland. It is unfortunately a short-lived peace, for Hemingway shows how those who rebel against society are ultimately punished for their actions. . . .

A Safari in Africa, a War in Spain

In the fall of 1933, Hemingway and Pauline left for a five-month African safari. Hemingway recounted their experiences in *Green Hills of Africa* (1935). While the book is about Africa, Hemingway discusses writing and writers in the early chapters. Here Hemingway makes his famous declaration that "all modern American literature comes from one book by Mark Twain called *Huckleberry Finn*." He probably said this because Twain was one of the first to use authentic, regional American speech in a work of literature. Huck Finn speaks like a real boy from Missouri, not like a character in a book. In fact, he is not so different from Nick Adams. Both are young men who rebel against society in order to find themselves and their own code.

Two short story masterpieces also came from Hemingway's African adventure: "The Snows of Kilimanjaro" and "The Short Happy Life of Francis Macomber." Both are stories of courage, betrayal, failure, and redemption.

To Have and Have Not (1937) Hemingway's third novel, and the only one set entirely in the Americas, attempts to show how the individual is easily corrupted in a world dominated by money. The theme of the novel is expressed by its hero: "A man alone ain't got no . . . chance." A similar theme is struck in Hemingway's immensely popular 1940 novel, *For Whom the Bell Tolls*, which takes place in Spain during the Spanish Civil War. Hemingway covered the war as a reporter, and it was in Spain that he met his third wife, the writer and journalist Martha Gellhorn.

The war was between those who favored a democratic republic and those who followed the fascist general Francisco Franco. Franco's side won and he ruled the country for more than forty years. Hemingway, like most American writers and intellectuals, was on the side of the republicans, also called the loyalists or the partisans. Hemingway's novel of the war centers on the American Robert Jordan and his love affair with a Spanish girl. The title of the book is taken from the writings of the seventeenth-century English poet John Donne. So is the theme of the book. Like the main character in *To Have and Have Not*, Robert Jordan comes to understand that all of us are "involved in mankind," and that "no man is an island."

Those who saw in the Spanish conflict forebodings of a second world war were right. Hemingway also covered World War II as a reporter. He is said to have helped Allied forces liberate Paris from Nazi control. During World War II, Hemingway met the journalist Mary Welsh. They were married and settled in Cuba, in a big house that Hemingway dubbed *Finca Vigia*, meaning "Lookout Farm." Here Hemingway enjoyed fishing from his boat *Pilar*, watching games of jai alai, and writing.

In 1954, Hemingway won the Pulitzer Prize for his short novel *The Old Man and the Sea* (1952). The old man of the title is a fisherman who struggles with, and learns to love, the marlin he chases for three days. The theme of the novel, "a man can be destroyed but not defeated," points to the nobility of all human beings. This short novel may also be one of Hemingway's best known. The Nobel Prize for literature went to the man by then known the world over as "Papa" Hemingway.

The Declining Years

But the 1950s were a rough time for America's most famous author. His health was in serious decline. Battered by two successive plane crashes in Africa and a life of heavy drinking, Hemingway suffered from a variety of physical problems over the next several years. But he continued to work on another book on bullfighting, *The Dangerous Summer*, his recollection of his years in Paris, *A Moveable Feast*, and a novel, *The Garden of Eden*. All were published after his death.

Following Fidel Castro's revolution, Cuba proved too unstable a country for Hemingway to live in. He and Mary moved to Idaho in 1960. Suffering from physical ailments and severe depression, Hemingway twice was secretly hospitalized in the Mayo Clinic in Rochester, Minnesota, where he received electroshock therapy.

He returned to Idaho but was unable to find relief from his depression. He felt that he could no longer write or participate in all the activities he used to enjoy. At seven o'clock in the morning of 2 July 1961, the Hemingway voice that had thrilled millions of readers was silenced forever by a self-inflicted gunshot.

Whatever flaws the man and the writer may have had, Hemingway was still able to influence the course of twentieth-century literature and culture. As the British critic and writer Anthony Burgess says, "Hemingway reminds us that to engage literature one has first to engage life."

The Inception and Reception of *A Farewell to Arms*

Robert W. Lewis

Robert W. Lewis was chair of the English Department at the University of North Dakota. He served as chair of the board of the Ernest Hemingway Foundation upon the request of Mary Hemingway, the author's fourth wife.

In the following viewpoint, Robert W. Lewis provides a glimpse into the writing process that gave birth to A Farewell to Arms *as well as a review of the novel's critical reception. Lewis claims Ernest Hemingway was at the height of his writing prowess when he penned* A Farewell to Arms *and notes that Hemingway seemed pleased with the results. Public reception, however, was divided. Lewis points out that some critics found the book too vulgar for popular tastes, yet others maintained its unsparing style was the novel's strength. Lewis also describes how specific aspects of the book—including its depiction of women and its potentially sentimental prose—have continued to inform modern criticism, proving that the significance of the work and its legacy are still an active part of American literary scholarship.*

A curious coincidence marked the publication of *A Farewell to Arms* in 1929. Another novel about World War I, Erich Maria Remarque's *All Quiet on the Western Front*, was also published in that year, but it describes the war from the point of view of a soldier on the other, the German, side. It was translated into English and was an immediate success and was eventually made into a fine motion picture. Hemingway's novel was published later in 1929, and as Remarque's novel

Robert W. Lewis, "The Inception and Reception of *A Farewell to Arms*," *Hemingway Review*, vol. 9, no. 1, Fall 1989, pp. 90–95. Copyright © 1989 by Hemingway Review. All rights reserved. Reproduced by permission.

was attracting so much attention, Hemingway was concerned about how the two novels would be compared. As it turned out, his novel also became a best seller and was made into a movie starring Gary Cooper (who became his friend) and Helen Hayes, two of Hollywood's leading stars.

Both novelists had participated in the Great War, and both had waited ten years before sorting out and articulating their experiences. Hemingway's first two novels, the short satire *The Torrents of Spring* (1926) and *The Sun Also Rises* (also 1926), were written quickly and soon after the events that had inspired them. The fine novel *The Sun Also Rises* stemmed from Hemingway's life in Paris in the 1920s and his holidays in Spain where he became a serious student of the bullfights. But even though the events both personal and public that formed the material for *A Farewell to Arms* had occurred in 1918, he had written only four short stories and several sketches that drew upon his wartime experiences (published in his first two collections of short stories *In Our Time* [1925] and *Men Without Women* [1927]).

In March 1928, however, he began writing what he "thought was only a story," as he wrote from Paris in a letter to his editor Maxwell Perkins. But in two weeks' time, the writing on it continued "wonderfully," and he "suddenly [got] a great kick out of the war and all the things and places and it has been going very well."[1] It had become the first draft of *A Farewell to Arms*. A month later, he was in Key West, Florida, with his second wife Pauline. He found that remote fishing village (population then only around ten thousand) a congenial place to work as well as to indulge his lifelong passion for fishing. In another letter to his editor, he again reported the writing on the new novel was "going very well," but when it was finished, he wanted to "put it away for a couple or three months and then re-write it. The re-writing doesn't take more than six weeks or two months once it is done. But it is pretty

Ernest Hemingway (center, right) in a trench with fellow war correspondents during the Spanish Civil War, circa 1937. © Daily Express/Hulton Archive/Getty Images.

important for me to let it cool off well before re-writing."[2] This description of his writing habits is sound advice for any writer, and it was essential for him to follow it in order to produce the tightly controlled, well-crafted writing of the finished novel.

Hemingway continued writing on the novel in Piggott, Arkansas, his wife's family home, that summer. Her pregnancy was difficult, and the baby was delivered by Caesarean section. "Pauline had a very bad time . . . and a rocky time afterwards. I was worried enough. Am now on page 486 . . . am going out to Wyoming . . . Will finish the book there."[3] This juxtaposition of news of the difficult birth with news of progress on the novel is at once amusing and yet an indication of how that birth is reflected in the novel set in far-off Europe ten years earlier, for the heroine Catherine dies in childbirth. The vivid rendering of the imagined scene had a painfully close counterpart in Hemingway's life at the very time he was writing the novel.

In Wyoming later that summer he wrote a letter with another amusing juxtaposition, this time a record of how many pages he had written on the novel and how many trout he had caught: "1st day–worked four pages, fished with Bill Horne caught 12. 2nd day–worked 4 1/2 pages, fished with two girls caught 2. 3rd day–worked zero, fished by self alone, caught 30-limit."[4] Nearing completion of the first draft, he seems to have had some self-doubt as to the quality of the novel; he thought he'd rather be in Spain following the bullfights, "instead of here trying to write. To hell with novels. . . ." But a few days later he read through all that he had written, almost six hundred manuscript pages, and he saw that it was "cockeyed wonderful."[5] By the end of August 1928, he had finished the first draft and was looking forward to rewriting the novel. He cautiously wrote his editor, "I believe maybe the book is pretty good [and I] have never felt better or stronger or healthier in the head or body—nor had better confidence or morale. . . ."[6] He had just written perhaps his best book, he was at the height of his powers, and his feelings were those of a rare peak experience.

By June of 1929, Hemingway had received the galley proof of the novel and was engaged in a friendly dispute with his editor Max Perkins over an aspect of the novel that would affect its critical reception. Hemingway was a writer of realistic fiction. One goal of his was to present stories based on life "the way it was" and not to romanticize or gloss over the rougher aspects of life. Since the subject matter included army life and a long hospital section, Hemingway's descriptions and dialog often used vulgar but realistic language that by latter-day standards would be commonplace. But even after reluctantly submitting to his editor's advice to prune or conceal with blanks possibly offensive language, the novel was criticized by some readers for its frankness. The old genteel tradition that Hemingway and others of his generation were rebelling against would not relent. The serialized version in

Scribner's Magazine (which was even more severely edited than the book version that would follow) was banned in Boston by the Superintendent of Police. A hoped-for sale to the Literary Guild or the Book-of-the-Month Club was abandoned, and the publisher and author rode out the storm of controversy, ultimately compromising by deleting or changing the then unprintable words like *balls* (for *testicles*), *f---*, and *shit*.

The tempest was, however, in a teapot in light of the reviews and sales that followed the publication of the book version in September 1929. Two reviewers wrote negatively about the novel, but one, Harry Hansen of the *New York World*, later reversed his opinion, possibly in light of the overwhelming flood of positive reviews. But another reviewer and fellow novelist, Robert Herrick, writing in the influential *Bookman* expressed the opinions of a significant audience at the end of the decade sometimes labeled the Roaring Twenties. In fact, there were many in the nation who reacted against realistic fiction that dealt with the often bitter truths of modern life. Herrick's review was titled "What Is Dirt?" The answer in his puritanical view was *A Farewell to Arms*. Even though the novel had been edited to meet Scribner's standards, the nation's taste was divided, and many readers still preferred not to be reminded of the "unpleasant garbage" of life (one of Herrick's phrases). To treat war and sex frankly was to run the risk of offending many readers. Herrick loftily admitted that he had read only half the novel, but that was enough for him to reach his conclusion.

Similarly, other readers of even the more severely edited magazine version wrote to Scribner's to complain and sometimes to cancel their subscriptions. To justify publication as catering to the "popular demand" or holding "the mirror up to nature" was insufficient reason because the vulgar mass of readers has no taste, and "indecency . . . may better be unrecognized" (as one offended reader wrote).[7]

To Hemingway, this criticism was not new. Indeed, he had faced it from his own parents upon the publication of his first book, *In Our Time,* in 1924. The copies he sent them they returned with their own Victorian astonishment that their son had somehow left the pious path they had led him on. He had defended himself in a letter to his father: "You see I'm trying in all my stories to get the feeling of the actual life across— not to just depict life—or criticize it—but to actually make it alive. . . . You can't do this without putting in the bad and the ugly as well as what is beautiful."[8] In a further irony, his father, seriously ill and in hard financial straits, had committed suicide between the time Hemingway had completed the novel and Scribner's had published it.

The best-seller status the novel earned was encouraged by the good reviews, for the majority of the reactions were very favorable. As if in answer to Hemingway's parents' and other puritanical readers' tastes, the very influential critic Henry Seidel Canby writing in the very important *Saturday Review of Literature* acknowledged that the novel was "an erotic story, shocking to the cold, disturbing to the conventional who do not like to see mere impersonal amorousness lifted into a deep, fierce love involving the best in both man and woman. . . . As for Hemingway's frankness of language, to object to it would be priggish. There is no decadence here, no overemphasis on the sexual as a philosophy."[9] Although one might wonder what he meant by that last phrase, the decade of the 20s was one of sexual liberation for some and of questioning about the very nature of human sexuality to many. Freud's ideas were in the air, and if no American was as bold as he, Americans knew about the British Havelock Ellis and Marie Stopes and the Dutch Theodoor Hendrik van de Velde whose books *The Psychology of Sex, Married Love, and Ideal Marriage* were frankly and practically addressing the problems of ignorance and repression.

Other influential critics like Malcolm Cowley and Clifton Fadiman also wrote favorable reviews. Hemingway, after all, had just turned thirty and was still a young man. Many readers no doubt wondered if this latest book fulfilled the promise of his earlier work which included two well-received collections of short stories and *The Sun Also Rises*. If early reviewers recognized talent and promise, later reviewers often raise their standards and demand more from the second novel than from the first. But in the case of both Cowley and Fadiman, they felt that Hemingway had surpassed himself and written his "best book to date . . . a remarkably beautiful book . . .[and] the very apotheosis of a kind of modernism."[10] Cowley took a different tack and saw the writing itself as "subtler and richer prose" appropriate to a changed attitude in which "emotions . . . are more colored by thought . . . [and are] more complicated" than in the earlier work.[11] Other reviewers as well often compared the new novel favorably with Hemingway's prior work, and considering the test of time in which, sixty years later, *A Farewell to Arms* continues to be so recognized, it is instructive to consider some of the details in that early critical reception.

The novel of course hasn't changed except in a few editorial details, but readers' tastes and perception do change. What was in today is out tomorrow, and vice versa, as we noted in respect to vulgate language. But other elements in the novel were early singled out for particular comment, and they continue to provide important foci for readers.

The heroine Catherine Barkley might be an enigma if one tried to understand her solely on the basis of criticism and not the novel itself. Some of the early reaction to the novel found her characterization one of the best features of the work. For instance, it "is a very fine portrayal of a woman who was not afraid."[12] But others compared her with Lady Brett Ashley, heroine of *The Sun Also Rises*, and found her selfless devotion to and love of the hero Frederic Henry hard to believe. Was she not merely a man's dream girl, little more than a far-fetched, romantic pasteboard figure? The early disagreement has continued to fuel discussions, and with the rise of feminist criticism an interesting reversal occurred. Most of the early critics who thought many of Hemingway's women characters tended to be either male-destroying bitches or characterless dream girls were male. Indeed, early in the new feminist movement of the 1970s, Hemingway seemed to many the epitome of the macho male who regarded and depicted women as either caretakers (housekeepers, cooks, button sewers) or sexual objects, but never as thinking and feeling individuals in their own right. This feminist reaction to Hemingway was fueled by the popular image of him, perhaps the most famous and familiar American author of all time. Photographs of him appeared on the covers and in the pages of mass-circulation magazines like *Time* and *Life*. He was often in hunting, fishing, boxing, bullfighting, or military scenes. Hollywood capitalized on and further promoted his fame as a tough guy, hard-boiled, forcefully sexual.

Although it was certainly true that in leisure time he enjoyed many sports, and as a journalist he covered wars in Europe and China, he was professionally a writer, and often an isolated, hardworking writer. But that person, the sensitive devotee of art, was not "good press."

Stimulated by feminist criticism, and notably by Judith Fetterley in *The Resisting Reader: A Feminist Approach to American Fiction*, Hemingway's work came to be reexamined in new perspectives.[13] In fact, Fetterley focused on Catherine Barkley of *A Farewell to Arms*, and in the decade since, several other books and numerous essays have been written by both men and women about Hemingway's women. Furthermore, a posthumously published novel by Hemingway himself (*The Garden of Eden*, 1986) revealed his interest in androgyny and his ability to characterize complex male-female relations. Perhaps the only safe conclusion one may reach about Hemingway's depiction of women in general and of Catherine Barkley in particular is that it is complex and ambivalent, and preconceptions of Hemingway's attitudes have almost certainly impeded the careful reading and understanding of the work.

Other important questions have been raised about the novel from the very first reviews of it. To what extent are the feelings of the characters well depicted? Dealing as it does with the elemental actions of battle and sexuality, strong emotions are inevitable, but in art a basic principle is that the depiction of feeling should be commensurate with the source or cause of it. If it is excessive or affected, we judge it to be sentimental and self-indulgent. However readers judge the balance between reason and emotion in this novel, clearly Hemingway did not shrink the risks of his subject.

Another debate opened by early reactions to *A Farewell to Arms* concerned the degree of success to which Hemingway blended the twin topics of love and war. Was it a war novel with a "romantic interest" or a love story set in wartime? If the former, some critics thought the virtual disappearance of the war from the last section of the novel a flaw. If it was centrally a love story, was not the emphasis on the male's experiences for long stretches and his first-person point of view a problem?

Hemingway's friend and fellow novelist John Dos Passos would expectedly emphasize the craft of the novel, which he praised, but also predictably, given the fact that his review was written for the socialist journal *New Masses*, he emphasized the political context of the novel (Dec. 1, 1929). Clearly another important and growing awareness of the protagonist Frederic Henry is of how the war is a class struggle, not of the Germans and Austrians versus the Italians and their allies, but of the *haves* versus the *have nots* in terms of power, money, distinction, rank. Looked at in this way, the novel takes on yet another dimension.

One critic, who later admitted his negative review used the novel as a whipping boy, read it as an illustration of the psychology of behaviorism in which the characters merely respond to external stimuli like a laboratory animal. They are "colorless" and "without souls," and although Hemingway's philosophy may echo science, it is a cruel guide to life.[14] On the other hand, charges of anti-intellectualism were raised against him. Although his characters seemed intelligent, they also seemed reluctant to think, and they evinced little culture. Wyndham Lewis' influential "The Dumb Ox: A Study of Ernest Hemingway" praised his style but criticized his primitivism, his almost total rejection of the life of the mind.[15]

Obviously, different readers approach works of literature with different tastes, different experiences, different hopes and expectations. The rich range of response to Hemingway's work reflects the breadth and power of the novel itself. It is not reducible to easy understanding from only one or two perspectives. Looked at from feminist, Marxist, psychological, and historical vantage points, the novel grows in our consciousness. Looked at from a narrow perspective, as it sometimes has been, the novel narrows.

The readings of *A Farewell to Arms* that have been generous in range and that see it centrally as a work of *art* (and not as a polemic for or against some *ideas*) have established it as a work of consummate writing craft, perhaps more profoundly *about* language and style themselves than about war or love. Language and its formed style are the materials with which Hemingway so carefully worked. That is not to say that this novel or any novel does not have a subject and ideas, and the greatness of *A Farewell to Arms* resides in part in the high seriousness of its subject of how one is to live well in a world of misrule and unreason. The vast majority of its readers have found some degree of understanding of life's dilemmas and tragedies in the well-wrought pages of this, one of the finest of modern novels.

Notes

1. *Selected Letters*, 273-74.

2. *Selected Letters*, 276-77.

3. *Selected Letters*, 280.

4. *Selected Letters*, 282.

5. *Selected Letters*, 283.

6. *Selected Letters*, 286.

7. As quoted in Michael S. Reynolds, *Hemingway's First War*, 83.

8. *Selected Letters*, 153.

9. October 12, 1929.

10. Clifton Fadiman, *The Nation*, October 30, 1929.

11. Malcolm Cowley, *New York Herald Tribune*, October 6, 1929.

12. "A.C.," *Boston Transcript*, October 19, 1929.

13. Bloomington: Indiana U.P., 1978.

14. Donald Davidson, *Nashville Tennessean*, November 3, 1929.

15. *Men Without Art*, London, 1934.

Social Issues
in Literature

CHAPTER 2

War in
A Farewell to Arms

A *Farewell to Arms* Glorifies War, Violence, and Masculinity

Lawrence R. Broer

Lawrence R. Broer is an English professor at the University of South Florida.

Two of the most well-known American authors of the twentieth century are Ernest Hemingway and Kurt Vonnegut; however, their portrayal of and stances on war have been seen as markedly different. In the following viewpoint, Lawrence R. Broer compares the novels A Farewell to Arms *and* Slaughterhouse-Five *and highlights the stark contrast between the two authors' treatment of war, violence, and masculinity. Broer argues that Hemingway's novel, while describing the carnage of war in gruesomely realistic detail, still glorifies the protagonist's role in war and venerates his masculine approach to dealing with the violence and death that surround him. According to Broer, Vonnegut opposed this view of war and strove to counter it both in his novels that recounted his experiences during World War II and in satirical responses to Hemingway's works. By illustrating the polarity between these authors' novels, Broer emphasizes the glorification of war, violence, and masculinity evident in* A Farewell to Arms.

Hemingway's work [*A Farewell to Arms*] constitutes a study of death and violence that amounts to a lesson in mortality, but if one counts deaths that are predicted or imagined as well as those that have actually occurred, there is a greater proliferation of corpses in [American author Kurt Vonnegut's] *Slaughterhouse-Five* than in any other twentieth-century novel.

Lawrence R. Broer, "Duty Dance with Death: A Farewell to Arms and Slaughterhouse-Five," *Vonnegut and Hemingway: Writers at War*. SC: University of South Carolina, 2011. Copyright © 2011 by University of South Carolina. All rights reserved. Reproduced by permission.

Though spared Frederic Henry's physical wound, [Vonnegut's protagonist] Billy Pilgrim is eventually driven mad by the killing machines of war, which tear and mutilate the body and create such sadistic creatures as the revenge-crazed Paul Lazzaro, who carries a list in his head of people he is going to have killed after the war, and the equally rabid Roland Weary, from whom Billy learns about wounds that will not heal, about "blood gutters" and such tortures as having your head drilled through with a dentist's drill, and about being staked to an anthill in the desert.

For both Frederic Henry and Billy Pilgrim, there comes a moment when the madness of war overwhelms them. For Henry, after the desperate retreat at Caporetto, any remaining notions of patriotism or devotion to duty are nullified by countless instances of cruelty, betrayal, and incompetence among his own fellow soldiers, climaxing in needless executions; Henry is mistaken for a German imposter and nearly executed himself. Overwhelmed by similar displays of human warpedness and injustice, Billy Pilgrim experiences a final unbalancing he likens to being stretched on the rack when he remembers the night Dresden was destroyed—the firestorm that "ate everything . . . that would burn, that turned the city into a desert and people into little petrified human beings."

Billy's experience consists of the same maddening contrasts between human ideals and the grotesque realities of war that force Frederic Henry to seek a separate peace and Helga Noth and Howard Campbell [the protagonists of Vonnegut's novel *Mother Night*] to retreat into their "Nation of Two": "bucolic interludes sandwiched between bouts of violence . . . and sanctioned public murder." Thus both men, as [American poet, author, and literary critic] Robert Penn Warren says of Frederic Henry, cut themselves from the confused world, which symbolically appears for Frederic as the routed army at Caporetto. When Frederic makes his baptismal plunge into the Tagliamento, he comes into the world of the man alone, no longer supported by and involved in society.

Masks Allow the Protagonists
to Escape and Survive

Threatened with annihilation and potentially disabled by fear and cynicism, the Hemingway and Vonnegut heroes face precisely the same dilemma: how to manage existential despair so great that insanity or suicide pose real threats. Billy and Frederic hunger for the sense of order and assurance that most seem to find in religious belief, but they cannot find grounds for such belief. How then do they avoid the complete dispiritedness for which they appear headed and retain faith in the value of human effort, which nevertheless dooms noble human beings such as Catherine Barkley [in *A Farewell to Arms*] and Edgar Derby [in *Slaughterhouse-Five*]? However, Warren and [American literary critic] Loree Rackstraw agree that for Frederic and Billy successfully confronting the existential void means more than personal survival. It means staying alive with decency in a world that has crippled them, giving moral significance to the confusions of living. It is how each author defines "moral significance" that divides them. Hemingway acquired ideas about how to live humanly, with courage and stoical bearing, from the world of the bullfight, a religious ceremony glorifying death and violence in the service of domination, whereas Vonnegut formulated ideas of conduct from Christ's Sermon on the Mount, adopting kindness and restraint as moral imperatives. The contrast seems striking in light of Hemingway's story "Today Is Friday," about Christ's Crucifixion. While the story says nothing about ideals of charity or compassion, it conspicuously praises Christ's manly bearing—his courage and ability to endure suffering. [American literature professor] Wendolyn Tetlow offers a useful way to distinguish the two modes of conduct. In Hemingway's case the world as essentially cruel and predatory is "accepted and

American actor Rock Hudson portrays Frederic Henry in the 1957 screen adaptation of Hemingway's A Farewell to Arms. © Mondadori Portfolio via Getty Images.

assimilated." Violence is justified because that is what it takes to prevail in a violent world, to prove that you are tougher and more courageous. Vonnegut chose to repudiate animal instinct, encouraging a loving rather than an adversarial relationship with nature.

Throughout *A Farewell to Arms* and *Slaughterhouse-Five*, however, the only way Billy Pilgrim and Frederic Henry find to deflect pain is to continue the dangerous evasive strategies of their younger selves, to retreat from consciousness and responsibility, which nullifies or at least postpones psychic healing. Frederic masks feelings of vulnerability behind a tough-guy stoicism that borders on cruelty, the schizophrenic fabrications of Pedro Romero and Jake Barnes [characters from Hemingway's *The Sun Also Rises*]; and Billy, his emotional fuses completely blown, practices a numbness of response that leaves him as robotically dazed and compliant as Howard Campbell. The authors' ironic, understated styles convey the protagonists' escape into what [Boston University English professor] Millicent Bell calls "the dreamless sleep of apathy"—a screen of simple words and short, declarative sentences meant to numb emotional pain and protect the hero from further horrors.

In their mutual strategies of disengagement from war, the adoption of false selves and dangerously escapist fantasy worlds is foreshadowed by the presence of playacting that Howard Campbell finds so lethal if taken as real, many instances of masquerading and game playing. Life is theater for Frederic, and Billy can relate only to imaginary scenes and people. In the prison-camp performance of "Cinderella," Cinderella's boots fit Billy perfectly—"Billy Pilgrim was Cinderella, and Cinderella was Billy Pilgrim." . . .

The Guilty Pleasures of Militarism

While Billy Pilgrim's disguises leave him dazed and without identity, his passivity seems in Vonnegut's view to be less morally objectionable than Frederic Henry's mask of stoical toughness, misogyny, and occasional cruelty. Apropos of Vonnegut's moral to *Mother Night*—that we are what we pretend to be—Frederic's soldierly masquerade becomes unnervingly real. What [English professor Thomas] Strychacz calls Henry's

"shifting articulations of identity" return us to Vonnegut's essential critique of *A Farewell to Arms* and to the authors' contrary views of what it means to fill the existential void "de-
cently" or "humanly." We have noted that in *Mother Night*
Vonnegut accuses Hemingway of glorifying war—of heroic
posing and the idealization of manly toughness—and of asso-
ciating honor with death and killing. Are these criticisms still
more pertinent to *A Farewell to Arms* and, if so, what do they
portend in understanding differences in each writer's vision of
life and war?

Certainly Hemingway's many descriptions of war wounds
in *A Farewell to Arms* portray war as anything but romantic or
glorious. Scenes showing the random horrors of death and
suffering on the battlefield not only rival but exceed Vonnegut's
in realistic detail. [English professor Linda] Wagner-Martin
points out that Hemingway's readers cannot escape the recognition of "relentless blood and dreadful death" and the frustration of medical knowledge to save lives. At the moment of
Frederic's own terrible wound, when he learns it was a mistake to think you just died, he describes the suffering of a particularly brave Italian soldier named Passini, hit by the same
trench-mortar shell: "His legs were toward me and I saw in
the dark and the light that they were both smashed above the
knee. One leg was gone and the other was held by tendons
and part of the trouser and the stump twitched and jerked as
though it were not connected." Passini screams in pain until,
Henry reports, "Then he was quiet, biting his arm, the stump
of his leg twitching." Henry tries in vain to make a tourniquet
but notices that Passini is "dead already. I made sure he was
dead." At the dressing station, Frederic sees doctors working
"red as butchers." After a doctor indifferent to Frederic's pain
finishes probing and bandaging his wounded knee, he finds
himself in an ambulance, placed beneath a hemorrhaging soldier in the cot above him. Frederic tries to move out of the
way, but cannot avoid the steady stream of blood from above,

turning him "warm and sticky." One would be hard-pressed to view Frederic Henry's famous denunciation of the usual base motivations for war, his contempt for the patriotic platitudes that send young men off to die, as less than a protest of war. When we hear the battle police during the retreat from Caporetto speaking of "the sacred soil of the fatherland" and the "fruits of victory" as they execute their own soldiers, we understand Frederic's disgust.

Yet, if there is validity to Thomas Strychacz's argument that Hemingway's episodes of war function as an alibi for the violence that is being celebrated, Vonnegut's concerns are not wholly misplaced. In Strychacz's view Hemingway's descriptions perform the double task of exploring the guilty pleasures of militarism, decrying, for instance, the pain of brave soldiers whose suffering and death nevertheless bring them glory. The merciless killings during the retreat are terrifying, certainly not an endorsement of the glory of battle or the nobility of death; yet they inspire in Henry exactly the self-conscious machismo Vonnegut disparaged in Harold Ryan [the main character in his play *Happy Birthday, Wanda June*], code-like exhibitions of toughness, bravery, and stoical fortitude, a markedly different response to war than that of Billy Pilgrim.

Frederic Henry Enjoys Killing

It is not difficult to view Frederic Henry's capacity for violence in light of Harold Ryan's assertion in *Happy Birthday, Wanda June*: "You've got to fight from time to time or get eaten alive." According to Robert Penn Warren and [American preacher, lecturer, and author] John Killinger, Frederic Henry's violence simply represents an appropriate response to "the great nada." Yet the naturally combative Frederic fights not only to survive, but because he likes it, taking pride in himself as a tough guy who enjoys intimidating other men and even inflicting pain. When he bloodies the face of an Italian officer with a single blow, takes pleasure in scaring the professor he boxes with in Lausanne, or relishes seeing the Italian artillery captain cower when he and Frederic want the same seat on a train, Frederic takes the same pride in his masculinity as he does watching himself shadowbox. There is little difference between this Frederic Henry and the Harold Ryan who thrives on physical threats and enjoys "twitting weaklings" or who proclaims that the core of his life was the pleasure of watching someone make the choice between fleeing and fighting—or of making the choice himself. "This is a moment of truth," Harold Ryan tells his buddy Shuttle contemptuously when Shuttle will not fight him, "and you're almost crying."

We know that when Frederic dispatches the suffering Passini, he acts from pity. But a far darker emotion surfaces—a seeming enjoyment of killing—when he shoots fleeing Italian officers who resist Henry's orders to help dig a car out of the mud. He describes the killing as coolly and indifferently as if he were shooting quail, consistent with an ideology of violence that increasingly desensitizes him and that he perversely enjoys. "I shot three times," he says, "and dropped one. The other went through the hedge and was out of sight." "Did I hit the other one at all?" he asks someone. When Bonello puts his pistol against the head of one of the fallen soldiers, Henry responds coldly, "You have to cock it."

If Vonnegut's portrait of Hemingway as the bellicose Harold Ryan indicts Hemingway for the kind of aggression that shows up in Frederic Henry, Ryan and Henry also share an unnerving propensity for heroic braggadocio. There are several episodes where Hemingway appears to undercut the kind of heroic posing Vonnegut detests. When Frederic says, "Nothing ever happens to the brave," Catherine smartly answers, "the brave die of course." Yet her view that the truly brave are quiet about it evokes a concept of heroic fortitude that seems staged and pretentious. We see that Frederic suffers, but his valor requires he deny its seriousness. When he describes his swollen and bleeding forehead as nothing, says he waits to have his knee wound dressed because there are much worse wounded, and understates the ordeal of the retreat on foot and then swimming the Tagliamento with "this knee," there is an unmistakable element of self-congratulation reminiscent of the false bravado of the British prisoners of war in *Slaughterhouse-Five*. Henry's shows of courage seem as stage managed for applause as Campbell's melodramas or Pedro Romero's feats of daring in the bullring.

Militancy and Masculinity Are Necessary in *A Farewell to Arms*

While Vonnegut's criticisms simplify complexities of text and characterization in *A Farewell to Arms*, they nevertheless illuminate essential differences in each writer's management of war wounds at almost identical phases of their careers. Vonnegut's suffering war hero Billy Pilgrim constitutes the antithesis of Hemingway's tough, violent, and sometimes brutal Frederic Henry. Like Norbert Woodly, Harold Ryan's peacenik counterpart in *Happy Birthday, Wanda June*, Pilgrim represents Vonnegut's dicta that "there's no time for battle, no point to battle any more." Woodly, Penelope says [in *Happy Birthday, Wanda June*], represents the new heroes who refuse to fight. "They're trying to save the planet." Billy's gentleness and subsequent refusal to participate in the world's destructiveness contrasts conspicuously with what we see of Frederic's truculence and enjoyment of physical confrontation. We see Billy as a latter-day Christ who cries at the sight of a suffering German horse, a moment that begs comparison with Hemingway's narrator's impersonal response to the crippled baggage animals thrown in the water to drown in "On the Quai at Smyrna."

Billy's natural gentleness and innocence, appropriate to his role as chaplain's assistant, hardly prepares him for the idiocy of battle, any more than Frederic Henry's boyish exuberance prepares him for war's destruction. Yet, if anything, Billy grows more docile, while Frederic becomes increasingly militant. While Frederic is self-consciously virile, Billy is loath to discover that his wife associates sex and glamour with war. Rather than show off his personal sexual prowess, Vonnegut jokes in the opening chapter that the war has made his own phallus inoperable—a "tool" that "won't pee anymore." All in all Billy experiences war as an interminable nightmare of victimization and madness in which everyone around him exhibits some form of insane, mechanically conditioned behavior. Hemingway's denunciations of war are more problematic, war viewed as a process of tempering the writer's craft and sensibility, a stage upon which to enact what Warren calls "the lessons of lonely fortitude," shows of courage and strength necessary to endure in a world that kills and maims with impunity.

A Farewell to Arms and Hemingway's Protest Stance: To Tell the Truth Without Screaming

William Dow

William Dow is an associate professor of comparative literature and English at the American University of Paris.

In the following viewpoint, William Dow traces a connection between A Farewell to Arms *and Henri Barbusse's* Le feu *(Under Fire), a French novel also about a volunteer serving in World War I. According to Dow, both works utilize a prose style that refrains from didacticism and opts instead to allow description and the words and observations of soldiers to convey the horrors of war. Dow insists these descriptions are not evidence of pure realism but are inflected with a poetic vernacular that distances* Farewell *from unadorned memoirs and novels that try to capture the grit of war. In addition, Dow claims that Hemingway, like Barbusse, holds old propagandist speech and traditional truths up for ridicule because these trite ideals ring hollow in the face of the traumas of modern war. In this way, Hemingway employs his poetic language and unsentimental descriptions to avoid clichés of the genre and to tell the truth about the war and the impact it had on the men who fought it.*

Hemingway's aesthetic connections to Henri Barbusse's *Le feu* (*Under Fire*) have been virtually ignored by American critics. But Hemingway appropriated in *A Farewell to Arms* Barbusse's method of "*constater*," his technique of suspending protest in "poetry," and his creation of a distinctly

William Dow, "A Farewell to Arms and Hemingway's Protest Stance: To Tell the Truth Without Screaming," *Hemingway Review*, vol. 15, no. 1, Fall 1995, pp. 72–87. Copyright © 1995 by Hemingway Review. All rights reserved. Reproduced by permission.

modern anti-war consciousness. Hemingway's introduction to *Men at War* (1942), while providing a qualified appreciation of *Le feu*, commends Barbusse's courage not to scream or write of individual heroism but to describe ordinary men in the extraordinary circumstances of World War I:

> The only good war book to come out during the last war was *Under Fire* by Henri Barbusse. He was the first to show us, the boys who went from school or college to the last war, that you could protest in anything besides poetry, the gigantic useless slaughter and lack of even elemental intelligence in generalship that characterized the Allied conduct of that war from 1915 to 1917.... But when you came to read it over to try to take something permanent and representative from it the book did not stand up. Its greatest quality was his courage in writing it when he did.... [Barbusse] had learned to tell the truth without screaming. (MAW $_9$)

Le feu brought the French novel back from a focus on aestheticism to the realm of a contemporary realism, but a realism infused with a new form of war protest and social criticism.[1] The degree that Barbusse and Hemingway privilege protest forms is the degree to which both writers necessarily disrupt their own narrativity and that of any linear history of the Great War. By analyzing *Le feu* and *Farewell* in reference to the linguistic concept of intertextuality, I hope to demonstrate a neglected source of Hemingway's protest stance.[2]

The links between Hemingway and Barbusse are literary and biographical as well as intertextual. Like Hemingway, Barbusse began his writing career as a journalist (reporting in the 1890s for the *Petit Parisien* and *Echo de Paris*) and his literary career as a poet (publishing in 1895 a collection of poems, *Pleureuses*). Both writers experienced the Great War, but Barbusse saw more combat than Hemingway did, serving for 22 months on the French fronts at Soissonnais, Argonne, and Artois. Both writers were invalided out. Barbusse began *Le feu* in a hospital in Chartres, where he was evacuated in January

1916, and finished it in a hospital in Plombières, 3 August 1916. If Roger Asselineau is even partially correct in asserting that "all Hemingway's so-called techniques were merely the systemization of methods which had already been used in the past by French writers" (61), Barbusse's *Le feu*, particularly by reason of its relationship to *Farewell*, deserves further study.[3]

Le feu uses a technique for writing that Hemingway retrospectively described as his own in "The Art of the Short Story": "So I do what the French call constater [and] that is what you must learn to do" (6). In his "*constater*," Barbusse, as Leo Weinstein puts it, "never preaches. He lets the soldiers and facts speak for themselves, and only at the end of the novel do the results of those experiences burst spontaneously out . . ."(71). "*Constater*," for Hemingway, involved a "boiling" down from which a condensed, authoritative, and "truthful" narrative emerges. But for both writers "*constater*" signaled a reappropriation of the "old words" of war propaganda and patriotism, carefully planned verbal patterns of protest (to elucidate the terms of the narrators' participation in the war), and a "poetic language" that includes what Ossip Brik has called a "transrational language."[4]

Le feu's "*constater*" was a corrective to the ineffectual war narratives of the time, which in France quickly began to appear hollow and unconvincing.[5] Barbusse, for example, avoiding the bombast of a Maurice Barrès (*Les bastions de l'est*) or the "heroic race" descriptions of a Drieu la Rochelle (*Gilles*), depicts life in the trenches simply and accurately. Barbusse returned to his roots of rationalism and positivism in *Le feu* by saturating his narrative in the "authentic" (a reliance on the "*constater*") as a protest and "moral" expression. As Frank Field has argued,

> . . . the best way in which [Barbusse] could serve the cause of peace in 1915 was not so much by attempting to convince men of the validity of the intellectual arguments against the war but by expressing his sense of moral outrage

at the events that were now taking place in Europe, by depicting, in as authentic a way as he could, the raw reality of the life at the front. It was by following this line of argument, therefore, that Barbusse came to produce *Le feu.* (*Three* 37)

In *Le feu's* last chapter, "*L'aube*," Barbusse's "*constater*" underscores his mistrust of an abstract and highly conceptualized language. Barbusse condemns, for example, the words that frequently appeared in the patriotic verse of the time:

> *Mais la gloire militaire, ce n'est même pas vrai pour nous autres, simples soldats. Elle est pour quelques-uns, mais en dehors de ces élus, la gloire du solat est un mensonge comme tout ce qui a l'air d'être beau dans la guerre.* (376) *Je leur dis que la fraternité est un rêve, un sentiment nuageux, inconsistant; qu'il est contraire à l'homme de haïr un inconnu . . .* (369)[6]

But in the closing paragraphs of "*L'aube*," after his book-long chronicle of "*la monotonie accablante et meurtrière des tranchées*," and for the common soldiers "*une sorte de fatalisme de la résignation ou du désespoir*" (Paraf 10), Barbusse attempts to give a new representational function to the formerly "deceitful" words ("*la vérité*," "*espoir*," "*force*," "*courage*"):

> *Mais leurs yeux sont ouverts. Ils commencent à se rendre compte de la simplicité sans bornes des choses. Et la vérité non seulement met en eux une aube d'espoir, mais aussi y bâtit un recommencement de force et de courage.*
>
> *—Assez parler des autres! commanda l'un d'eux. Tant pis pour les autres! . . . Nous! Nous tous! . . .* (377–8)[7]

Because here the "old" words come from the voices and consiousness of the "simples soldats," "*constater*" takes a more forceful protest form: its targets are now the war profiteers and the immense suffering of "*la multitude, invisible et silencieux*" (Carnet 458).

In *Farewell*'s "*constater*," Frederic likewise condemns "abstract words such as glory, honor, courage, or hallow [which] were obscene beside the concrete names of villages, the numbers of roads, the names of rivers, the numbers of regiments and the dates" (191). But echoing *Le feu*'s alternative to the "old" signifiers, *Farewell* ambiguously slides from one representational paradigm to another. Frederic's desertion, subsequent arrival in Milan, and making of his "separate peace" lead to a new appropriation of the "obscene" words.[8] Words such as "courage," "good," "gentle," and "brave" are now applied to the (ostracized, defeated) victims of war, and thereby, for Frederic, lose their former meanings:

> If people bring so much *courage* to this world the world has to kill them to break them, so of course it kills them. The world breaks everyone and afterwards many are strong at the broken places. But those that will not break it kills. It kills *the very good* and *the very gentle* and *the very brave* impartially. (258–9, my emphasis)

For the first time in *Farewell*, Frederic uses such terms unironically, appropriately enough after his escape in which "anger was washed away in the river along with any obligation" (240). From this point on in *Farewell*, the protest exfoliates towards the conspiratorial "they" and "the world," a protest, though, now containing the newly valorized words. Through such social and linguistic representations, Hemingway's dark vision is thus, at least temporarily, transformed into a veritable mode of "re-seeing." On this level, in the full modernist problematic of "the precariousness of the links between the traditional forms of representations and the eroding relations of representativeness" (Weimann 442), both texts (extraordinarily) appropriate the dominant language of war propaganda and politics.

But a buildup of protest precedes the reappropriation. *Le feu*'s first chapter, "*La vision*," sets a pattern of protest that Hemingway follows in *Farewell*. Barbusse, for instance, constantly shifts from lyrical descriptions of nature to the impending or actual destructions of landscape:

> *Les étendues calmes du vallon orné de villages roses comme des rose et de pâturages veloutés, les taches magnifiques des montagnes, la dentelle noire des sapins et la dentelle blanche des neiges éternelles, se peuplent d'un remuement humain.* (2–3)

The next paragraph in "*La vision*" provides a graphic contrast:

> *Des multitudes fourmillent par masses distinctes. Sur des champs, des assauts, vague par vague, se propagent, puis s'immobilisent; des maisons sont éventrées comme des hommes, et des villes comme des maisons, des villages apparaissent en blancherus émiettées comme s'ils étaient tombés du ciel sur la terre, des chargements de morts et des blessés épouvantables changent la forme des plaines.* (3)[9]

The pattern continually repeats itself, either at the beginning of a chapter, as in two ("*le grand ciel pâle*," 6), three ("*l'aube grisâtre*," 51), or nineteen ("*l'immensité de la brume*," 222), or functioning within a given chapter, as in five (67–68), twelve (159), fourteen (184), or twenty-four (352–53). Barbusse's characteristic pattern sets up a double-voiced discourse that simultaneously rejects the purpose of war as it accepts the reality of war's intrusion.

Farewell follows a similar formula, as seen in Frederic's description of the Austrian mountains at the end of chapter eight:

> Then, as the road mounted along the ridge, I saw a third range of mountains, higher snow mountains, that looked chalky white and furrowed, with strange planes, and then there were mountains far off beyond all these that you could hardly tell if you really saw. Those were all the Austrians' mountains and we had nothing like them. (47)

The next scene provides a sharp contrast with a landscape blighted by the encroaching forces:

Ahead there was a rounded turn-off in the road to the right and looking down I could see the road dropping through the trees. There were troops on this road and motor trucks and mules with mountain guns and as we went down, keeping to the side, I could see the river far down below, the line of ties and rails running along it, the old bridge where the railway crossed to the other side and across, under a hill beyond the river, the broken houses of the little town that was to be taken. (47)

The alternate scenes of uninhabited or untouched nature and nature destroyed by war recur, for example, in chapters two (5–6), three (10), eight (46–47), twenty-seven (191), and in all chapters involving troop movements (twenty-eight, twenty-nine), or the results of a battle (thirty). Asserted in these patterns, both novels suggest that the condition of a nature destroyed further diminishes the self, and that the silence of nature, while inducing a deferential respect in the survivors, serves the memory of the victims.

Barbusse's descriptions of untouched nature shifting to the effects of war on nature also work on the sentence level. The immense stillness of "*des sometueuses prairies où luisent doucement les vaches vernissées, et les bois noirs, et les champs verts, et les distances bleues*" cannot hold back the "storm" of war:

Mais quand le soir prépare à venir dans la vallée, un orage éclate sur le massif du Mont-Blanc. Arrêter la guerre! disent-ils. Arrêter les orages! (4)[10]

Hemingway's protests also work at the sentence level. When Frederic, for example, returns to the front at the beginning of chapter three, the phrase "and spring had come" is appended to the description of "many more guns in the country around"(12). In chapter three, Hemingway furthers his pattern of protest by condensing his descriptive contrasts of nature (A) and war (B) in these consecutive sentences:

A) I saw the town with the hill and the old castle above it in a cup in the hills with the mountains beyond, brown mountains with a little green on their slopes.

B) In the town there were more guns, there were some new hospitals, you met British men and sometimes women, on the street, and a few more houses had been hit by shell fire.

A) It was warm and like the spring and I walked down the alleyway of trees, warmed from the sun on the wall, and found we still lived in the same house and that it all looked the same as when I had left it.

B) The door was open, there was a soldier sitting on a bench outside in the sun, an ambulance was waiting by the side door and inside the door, as I went in, there was the smell of marble floors and hospital. (10)

To end the pattern, Hemingway conflates in a single sentence Frederic's sense of helplessness ("It was all as I had left it . . .") with the fact that "now it was spring" (10). As in *Le feu*, the truth-telling protest draws its power from syntactical patterns of perception and moral imagination. Hemingway's "extraordinary actuality" (Stevens 411), his technique of making every act, dialogue, or event seem urgently portentous, depends on these carefully crafted sentences.

Reading *Farewell* as a protest narrative depends, however, on the reader refusing to consider the text as a single unit and its constituent parts as objects in themselves. Rather, as an intertextual approach insists, "every text is a network of texts, replete with echoes of earlier texts, with no necessarily isolable locus of value or meaning" (Payne and Fleming, 12). For *Farewell*, *Le feu* is an important part of this network: a prototype of a genre that remains important and a chronicle, however structurally flawed, that does not scream.

Serviceable to another form of protest in both novels is a primary organizing principle of modernism: the awareness of not only the narrator as the lyrical subject, but also of the provisional or hypothetical nature of his or her point of view. This dynamic is evidenced in the pronominal shifts of both novels. In *Le feu*, the shifts begin in chapter two, where the narrator changes from the first person pronoun "I" ("*Je vois des ombres émerger de ces puits latéraux . . .*" 7) to the collective "we ("*Nous sommes emmitouflés à la manière des populations artiques . . .*" 7). The rest of the novel is essentially devoted to identifying the "we," beginning with the questions "*Nos âges?*," "*Nos races?*," "*Nos métiers?*" (16–18). But the narrator frequently shifts from the "we" to the "I" as a kind of stepping back device, both to report the devastation of war and to separate himself from it. (Hemingway's "I/you" pronominal shifts, as we shall see, serve a similar purpose.) Through these shifts the narrator of *Le feu* becomes part of a larger, gradually defined group. Thus as individual identities are brought to the foreground, a rejection of the war solidifies, and a common enemy emerges:

> . . . [T]ous ces gens-là qui ne peuvent pas ou ne veulent pas faire la paix sur la terre; tous ces gens-là, qui se cramponnent, pour une cause ou pour une autre, à l'état de choses ancien, lui trouvent des raisons ou lui donnent, ceux-là sont vos ennemis! (375)[11]

Le feu concludes, as does *Farewell* with its conspirational "they," that the isolated "*ils*," or "*tous ces gens-là*," are responsible for the causes and conditions of war. The point of view in both novels provides a tension between an abstract rendering of the war and war as a composite of the experiencing self. Both notions reinforce a similar artistic position: the modernist outlook "that views art entirely in terms of its making and the literal results of that making" (Kuspit 51).

Farewell essentially inverts the pronominal shifts of *Le feu* while consistently maintaining its protest form. The first chapter begins with the pronoun "we," identifying presumably those who live in that "house in a village" (3). The first shift in narrative voice takes place in chapter two, where the focus narrows to Frederic's individual responses and feelings. In chapters three and four there is some vacillation between the "I" and "we," but in succeeding chapters the "I" eventually dominates. Several critics have interpreted the pronominal shifts as an issue of Frederic's "uncertain identity" or Hemingway's deliberate "opacity," or as a deferral and multiplication of Frederic's "identities."[12]

While these interpretations appear valid, I would rather stress, as an additional protest pattern, aspects of the "I/you" and the "you/they" pronominal shifts. Just prior to his desertion at the end of chapter thirty, Frederic states, "They [the Italian battle police] were all young men and they were saving their country" (233) and then comments on the executions: "The questioners had that beautiful detachment and devotion to stern justice of men dealing in death without being in any danger of it" (233). (Barbusse essentially makes the same argument in "*L'aube*," preceding the symbolic "desertion" of the French soldiers from the collective cause, 376.) Significantly, the pronominal shift from "I" to "you" occurs during Frederic's desertion: "You do not know how long you are in a river when the current moves swiftly" (235) and then, in chapter thirty-two, intensifies in relation to his resolve to "abandon" the war completely: "you" appears as a subject, for example, eight times in the third paragraph in this pivotal chapter.

The "I/you" pronominal shift occurs most frequently when Frederic either wants to remember or reject something. He wishes to remember, for example, his time with Catherine in a Milan hospital ("... *you* would hear the ice against the pail ... it was dark afterward and *you* went to the window," 39, my emphasis). But "you" as a subject (and verbal device of Frederic's contemplations) is most effectively used in protest form. After escaping from the battle police, and boarding a train to Milan, Frederic/the narrator makes the "I/you" pronominal shift:

You saw emptily, lying on your stomach, having been present when one army moved back and another came forward. You had lost your cars and your men as a floorwalker loses the stock of his department in a fire. There was, however, no insurance. You were out of it now. You had no more obligation. (241)

The "you" indicates Frederic's belief that he can share his loss of identity as a soldier and separate himself from the war. But he also comments on the absurdity of war ("having been present when one army moved back and another came forward") and the impossibility of the individual (the "I") to make any kind of substantive difference.

The most emphatic use of the pronominal shift occurs in the last chapter, where Frederic, following the shift, combines the "you" with the conspiratorial "they":

Now Catherine would die. That was what you did. You died. You did not know what it was about. You never had time to learn. They threw you in and told you the rules and the first time they caught you off base they killed you. Or they killed you gratuitously like Aymo. Or gave you syphilis like Rinaldi. But they killed you in the end. You could count on that. Stay around and they would kill you. (338)

As in *Le feu*, *Farewell* ends with the (more subtle) assertion that there is a terrible injustice perpetrated by those ("they") who do not feel its effects. The real enemies, as in *Le feu*, are inexplicable suffering and death, and a sociopolitical system that allows war to take place. *Farewell*, in this way, asserts its intertextuality and partially defines itself through the patterned presence of elements from the earlier *Le feu*.

But Hemingway goes beyond these protest patterns in *Farewell* to permeate the text with a distinctly "poetic language."[13] To put it another way, *Farewell* is a response in poetic essences against the traditional realistic war novel, against a realism inadequate for creating a "modern" protest narrative. Critics have commented extensively on how the language in

Farewell is based on the rhythms of speech and a metaphysical precision of detail. However, in *Farewell* the language also inhabits a wider "language of essences," and is predicated on "a substitution of the image for the world" (Bonnefoy 126). Evincing in its cumulative effect a "larger picture" of protest, the language creates a succession of episodic, self-directed details rather than a realistic version of chronology. As James Nagel has recently observed, *Farewell* is fundamentally not a realistic narrative about World War I, but needs to be "tempered by a fresh reading of the novel as a work of art" (171). Frederic's voice, and his purpose for telling his story, emphasize much more than "coming to terms emotionally with the events" (Nagel 171). By objecting to the real effects of war, the voice constantly relies on protest images, creating a certain durational rhythm that goes far beyond the personal.

Self-negating capsules of nostalgia for an untouched and unchanging present, the poetic protests in *Le feu* and *Farewell* elucidate the humanity of their subjects and the inhumanity of war. In *Le feu*, Barbusse, prefacing his first dialogue, and thereafter employing a poetic frame, introduces his subject:

> *Peu à peu, les hommes se détachent des profondeurs. Dans les coins, on voit de l'ombre dense se former, puis ces nuages humains se remuent, se fragmentent. . . On les renonnaît un à un.* (8)[14]

Part of a system generated by the narrator within the specific social and historical fields of war, this framing device is used to describe the beginning or end of a time period (*"Le crépuscule du soir arrivait du côté de la campagne. Une brise douce, douce comme des paroles, l'accompagnait,"* 139), an action (229–30), or an event (239). The poetic language in both novels complements the *"constater"* of the warring soldiers, thereby liberating the subject of protest from any number of linguistic, social, and political categories. It generally forms, as Brik has emphasized, a transrational language that subverts the idea that poetic function must be limited to poetry, or that poetry must be restricted to the poetic function.[15]

Before introducing characters or presenting dialogue, Hemingway protests through his poetic descriptions. As in *Le feu*, the forces of nature reveal the location of the soldiers going to war:

> The forest of oak trees on the mountain beyond the town was gone. The forest had been green in the summer when we had come into the town but now there were the stumps and the broken trunks and the ground torn up, and one day at the end of the fall when I was out where the oak forests had been I saw a cloud coming over the mountain. It came very fast and the sun went a dull yellow and then everything was grey and the sky was covered and the cloud came on down the mountain and suddenly we were in it and it was snow. (6)

Hemingway resorts to this (prefatory) device of poetic language, standing in opposition to functional description or spoken language in, for example, chapters two (5–6), three (10), eleven (71), and twenty-five (169). Hemingway, like Barbusse, thus reinforces the ambiguity of thought and reason for war (disruption is a confirmation of authenticity) while commenting on the degradation of war's effects.

Le feu is in fact a protest that uses language to realize the possibilities inherent in a "poetic language." Often dismissed as a mere political tract, *Le feu*, as Tobin H. Jones has argued, "is richest in its implications as an artistic and social statement when studied from a literary rather than an ideological perspective" (217). Barbusse's war experiences take the form of a poeticity—depicting of "truth" as a series of images or impressions and substituting "mythical" for "realistic" descriptions. To create his poetic effect, Barbusse frequently combines natural and military imagery:

> *Le autres hommes de garde, promenant leurs regards braqués dans l'espace, contemplent deux avions ennemis et l'écheveau*

embrouillé de leurs lacis. Autour des oiseaux mécaniques et rigides, qui suivent le jeu des rayons, apparaissent dans les hauteurs, tantôt noirs comme des corbeaux, tantôt blancs comme des mouettes—des multitudes d'eclatements de shrap-nells pointillent l'azur et semblent une longue volée de flacons de neige dans le beau temps. (89)[16]

Le feu and *Farewell* are similarly concerned with the presence of a poetic language (be it French nineteenth-century symbolist poetry, characterized by specific mythic traditions, or a prose imbued with the devices of Anglo-modernist poetry). The lyricism of both novels not only envelops the immense sadness and injustice of the war but, informed by the drives of Frederic and the soldiers of the 231st regiment, serves as a boundary, a barrier, a temporary resistance to it. Poetic language is the reason why these authors came up with similar views of the war and similar ways of presenting those views.

As stated in the introduction to *Men at War, Le feu* showed Hemingway that a cogent, conclusive protest could only take the form of "poetry." This aesthetic, of course, never left him, for he constantly returned to the idea that the novelist, regardless of his or her intention, must begin with poetry:[17]

> Nobody really knows or understands and nobody has ever said the secret. The secret is that it is poetry written into prose and it is the hardest of all things to do. . . . (in *On Writing* 4)

Although *Le feu* is hardly a major literary precursor to *Farewell* and its importance is minor in the canon of Hemingway influences, the French novel is significant for the development of Hemingway's technique of protest against the Great War. Barbusse and Hemingway, journalists instilled in the literary traditions of naturalism and symbolism, realized that the truth of their personal experiences would best be rendered atemporal. Words and their composition must not be mere representations of the objects named, or indifferent references to reality, but must acquire a value, a weight of their own.

Thus, in their episodic forms *Le feu* and *Farewell* follow documentable origins, but are not "realistic" or journalistic accounts. Hemingway and Barbusse give their novels chronological order without stressing causal, spatio-temporal relationships among the events. In the process, they create a world of suffering and absurdity in which natural events and humanity's irrational actions collide. Both novels demand that the reader move to an intuitive, atemporal mode of inquiry in order to understand the protest patterns and language of this world. Hemingway, perhaps after all, did "take something permanent and representative" from *Le feu*. *Farewell*, in the wake of *Le feu's* contravention of conventional war narratives, not only suggests the inevitable human consequences created by the Great War, but points to a significantly new way to tell the truth without screaming.

Notes

1. When the trend of aestheticism began to fade at the end of the 1890s, French literature once more began to involve itself in social criticism. Barbusse's *Le feu* (1916) and Roland Dorgeles' *Les croix de bois* (1919) brought the French novel abruptly back into contact with contemporary social reality. Barbusse's primary objective, as Mary Jean Green has noted, "was the simple imperative of communication: the need to explain the reality of life in the trenches to a civilian population whose view of war had been shaped by 19th-century mythologies and more recent wartime propaganda" (850). Yet literary allusion, the development of a poetic mythology, and the concentration on rendering only images are often, in *Le feu*, the modes of Barbusse's social criticism.

2. Michael Payne and Richard Fleming, in *Criticism, History, and Intertextuality*, say "intertexuality is born with the recognition that a given text uncannily refuses to obey the principle of organic form by assuming the shape of a unified whole, however fissured by irony, tension, and paradox. From the beginning, intertextuality extends through the recognition of dialogic voices of other texts echoing within every text" (12).

3. Michael Reynolds notes in *The Young Hemingway* that much of Hemingway's juvenilia was filled "with slang phrases and newly acquired interests" (90). Many of these interests stayed with Hemingway and later resurfaced in his more mature work. In an early story, "The Woppian Way" (1919), Hemingway named one of his characters Henri Barbusse, indicating his then current interest in the French

writer. In Milan, shortly before writing "Woppian Way," Hemingway had read the 1918 Everyman edition of *Le feu*, translated by Fitzwater Wray. I have taken the English translations of *Le feu* from the 1918 edition.

4. For Ossip Brik and others of the Society for the Study of Poetic Language in Moscow (1917), "'poetic language' stands in opposition to spoken language whose basic purpose is communication." But I posit that the "poetic language" in *Farewell* and *Le feu* should not be viewed as a deviation from the norms of language or as a sub-code of the linguistic code. See Leon S. Roudiez's discussion of poetic discourse in Julia Kristeva's *Revolution in Poetic Language* (2–3).

5. For war narratives in France, see Frank Field's commentary in *British and French Writers of the First World War*. On the ideological and political function of *Le feu*, see Field's *Three French Writers and the Great War* (25–37) and Jonathan King's "Henri Barbusse: *Le feu* and the Crisis of Social Realism" in *The First World War in Fiction: A Collection of Critical Essays* (43–52).

6. "But military glory—it isn't even true for us common soldiers . . . the soldier's glory is a lie, like every other fine-looking thing in war" (Wray 341). "I tell them that fraternity is a dream, an obscure and uncertain sentiment; that while it is unnatural for a man to hate one whom he does not know, it is equally unnatural to love him" (Wray 336).

7. "But their eyes are opened. They are beginning to make out the boundless simplicity of things. And Truth not only invests them with a dawn of hope, but raises on it a renewal of strength and courage." 'That's enough talk about the others!' one of the men commanded; 'all the worse for them!—Us! Us all!' (Wray 342).

8. In a dialogue which precedes his admission that he has "perhaps . . . outlived [his] religious feeling," Count Greffi recommends that Frederic read *Le feu* (FTA 270, 272). Hemingway, significantly, places the discussion of *Le feu* shortly after Frederic's desertion from the Italian army.

9. "The tranquil expanses of the valley, adorned with soft and smooth pastures and hamlets rosy as the rose, with the sable shadow-stains of the majestic mountains and the black lace and white of the pines and eternal snow, become alive with the movements of men. Attacks develop, wave by wave, across the fields and then stand still. Houses are eviscerated like human beings and towns like houses. Villages appear in crumpled whiteness as though fallen from heaven to earth. The very shape of the plain is changed by the frightful heaps of the wounded and slain" (Wray 2).

10. "But when evening is ready to descend within the valley, a storm breaks over the mass of Mont Blanc. . . . 'Put an end to war?' say the watchers.—'Forbid the Storm!'" (Wray 3).

11. "They distort even truth itself. For the truth which is eternally the same they each substitute their national truth. So many nations, so many truths; and thus they falsify and twist the truth. All those people are your enemies!" (Wray 340).

12. See for example Peter Messent, Ernest Hemingway (56–63); Gerry Brenner, Concealments in Hemingway's Works (35); and Ben Stoltzfus, "A Sliding Discourse: The Language of *A Farewell to Arms*," in *New Essays on A Farewell to Arms* (109–110).

13. Critics have undervalued Hemingway's early training in poetry. In 1923, however, Harriet Monroe, then the editor of *Poetry: A Magazine of Verse*, first tagged Hemingway a "young Chicago poet" (*Poems xi*), who was soon to publish his first book of verse (*Three Stories and Ten Poems*, 1923). Ezra Pound, in recommending Hemingway as an editor for the *Transatlantic Review*, told Ford Madox Ford that "[Hemingway] writes very good verse and he's the finest prose stylist in the world" (Baker 7). Wallace Stevens in 1942 considered Hemingway's work to be the "poetry of extraordinary actuality" and thought of Hemingway as "the most significant of living poets" under this category (411–12). Pound and Stevens rightly connected Hemingway's minor poetic talents with his considerable gift for poeticizing the actual.

14. "I see shadows coming from these sidelong pits and moving about, huge and misshapen lumps, bear-like, that flounder and growl. They are 'us'" (Wray 5–6).

15. See Roman Jakobson, *Essais de linguistique generale* (218).

16. "The other men on guard, their concentrated gaze roaming in space, watch two enemy airplanes and the intricate skeins they are spinning. Around the stiff mechanical birds up there that appear now black like crows and now white like gulls, according to the play of the light, clouds of bursting shrapnel stipple the azure, and seem like a long flight of snowflakes in the sunshine" (Wray 81).

17. See Linda Wagner's comments on the writing of the 1920s, particularly her section on genreless forms and "the transfer of principles and devices from one mode to another," in *The Modern Novel: 1914–1945* (27–28).

18. Pertinent to Hemingway's advice in "The Art of the Short Story"—"You should learn French if you are going to understand short stories and there is nothing rougher than to do it all the way" (6)—the French poet Yves Bonnefoy has been struck by the aptitude of the English language for noting appearances, for "describing what consciousness perceives, while avoiding any preconceptions about the final being of these referents." English poetry can enter "the world of the relative, of meanings, of ordinary life, in a way almost unthinkable in the 'most sublime' French poetry" (126), which is given to the reestablishment of "openness" and "a substitution of the image for the world" (171). French literary language, as Bonnefoy perceives it, "connote for the most part not empirically determined appearances but entities seeming to exist in themselves. . ." (127).

Works Cited

Asselineau, Roger. *The Literary Reputation of Hemingway in Europe*. New York: New York U P, 1965.

Baker, Carlos. *Ernest Hemingway: A Life Story.* New York: Scribner's, 1969.

Barbusse, Henri. *Le feu.* Paris: Flammarion, 1916.

———. *Carnet de Guerre.* Rptd. in *Le feu* by Henri Barbusse. Paris: Flammarion, 1965.

Bonnefoy, Yves. *The Act and Place of Poetry.* Chicago: U of Chicago P, 1989.

Brenner, Gerry. *Concealments in Hemingway's Works.* Columbus: Ohio State U P, 1993.

Field, Frank. *British and French Writers of the First World War.* Cambridge: Cambridge U P, 1991.

———. *Three French Writers and the Great War.* Cambridge: Cambridge U P, 1975.

Fleming, Richard and Michael Payne. *Criticism, History, and Intertextuality.* London: Bucknell U P, 1988.

Green, Mary Jean. "Visions of Death and Dissolution." *A New History of French Literature.* Ed. Denis Hollier. Cambridge, MA: Harvard U P, 1984. 850–855.

Hemingway, Ernest. "The Art of the Short Story." 1959. *New Critical Approaches to the Short Stories of Ernest Hemingway.* Ed. Jackson J. Benson. Durham: Duke U P, 1990.

———. *88 Poems.* Ed. Nicholas Gerogiannis. New York: Harcourt Brace, 1979.

———. *A Farewell to Arms.* New York: Scribner's, 1929.

———. *Men at War.* New York: Crown, 1942.

———. *On Writing.* Ed. Larry W. Phillips. New York: Scribner's, 1984.

Jakobson, Roman. *Essais de linguistique generale.* Paris Minuit, 1963.

Jones, Tobin H. "Mythic Vision and Ironic Allusion: Barbusse's *Le feu* and Zola's *Germinal*." *Modern Fiction Studies* 28.2 (Summer 1982): 215–228.

King, Jonathan. "Henri Barbusse: *Le feu* and the Crisis of Social Realism." *The First World War in Fiction: A Collection of Critical Essays*. Ed. Holgar Klein. New York: Harper and Row, 1977. 43–52.

Kristeva, Julia. *Revolution in Poetic Language*. Ed. Leon S. Roudiez. New York: Columbia U P, 1984.

Kuspit, Donald. "The Unhappy Consciousness of Modernism." *Zeitgeist in Babel*. Ed. Ingeborg Hoesterey. Bloomington: Indiana U P, 1991.

Messent, Peter. *Ernest Hemingway*. New York: Macmillan, 1992.

Nagel, James. "Catherine Barkley and Retrospective Narration in *A Farewell to Arms*." *Ernest Hemingway: Six Decades of Criticism*. Ed. Linda Wagner. East Lansing: Michigan State U P, 1987. 171–193.

Paraf, Pierre. "Preface." *Le feu* by Henri Barbusse. Paris: Flammarion, 1965.

Reynolds, Michael. *The Young Hemingway*. New York: Basil Blackwell, 1986.

Robert, Paul. *Le Petit Robert 1*. Eds. A. Roy and J. Roy-Deboue. Paris: Le Robert, 1987.

Stevens, Wallace. *The Letters of Wallace Stevens*. Ed. Holly Stevens. New York: Knopf, 1961.

Stoltzfus, Ben. "A Sliding Discourse: The Language of *A Farewell to Arms*." *New Essays on A Farewell to Arms*. Ed. Scott Donaldson. Cambridge: Cambridge U P, 1990.

Wagner-Martin, Linda. *The Modern American Novel 1914–1945*. Boston: Twayne, 1990.

Weimann, Robert. "Text, Author-Function, and Appropriation in Modern Narrative: Towards a Sociology of Representation." *Critical Inquiry.* 14.3 (Spring 1988). 431–447.

Weinstein, Leo. *The Subversive Tradition in French Literature.* Vol. 2. Boston: Twayne, 1989.

Wray, Fitzwater. Trans. *Under Fire* by Henri Barbusse. London: Everyman, 1918.

Hemingway's Complex Meditation on the Evils of War and the Nobility of Soldiers

Erik Nakjavani

Erik Nakjavani is a professor of humanities at the University of Pittsburgh.

In the following viewpoint, Nakjavani argues that Ernest Hemingway had a complex attitude toward warfare. To Nakjavani, A Farewell to Arms *and other works expose war as an evil perpetrated on nations by governments and profiteers who are often untouched by its tragedies. However, Nakjavani contends that Hemingway did believe that there is merit in fighting wars to oppose domination or authoritarian oppression because freedom is always preferable to slavery. Nakjavani also notes that while Hemingway condemned war as a criminal act, he never indicted the soldiers who fought. He explains that Hemingway viewed bravery in combat and enduring the rigors of the soldier's life as admirable qualities that teach men about life and death.*

Hemingway's 1949 preface to the illustrated edition of *A Farewell to Arms* (1929) gives him the opportunity to express his views on the topic of war as a persistent dimension of the human condition. "The title of this book is *A Farewell to Arms*," he writes, "and except for three years there has been war of some kind almost ever since it has been written." Considering the enormity of the subject, Hemingway's tone is relatively disillusioned, reticent, and almost detached, without heat or hope, but authoritative. He makes a simple statement

Erik Nakjavani, "Hemingway on War and Peace," *North Dakota Quarterly*, vol. 68, no. 2–3, Spring–Summer 2001, pp. 245–73. Copyright © 2001 by Erik Nakjavani. All rights reserved. Reproduced by permission.

that may be boiled down to stating that the lived history of our time is experiential proof of the inevitability of war. He only intimates that the title refers to his World War I (1914–1918) novel, a war of unprecedented mechanized violence and brutality, which was naively hailed by some as the war to end all wars. The intervening years, before and after the publication of *A Farewell to Arms*, were to belie that claim. Wars and other conflicts betrayed even the most modest measure of hope the title in one of its multiple significations might have implied—both on the planes of the individual and the particular and the national and the universal. The three years of uneasy peace to which Hemingway refers could have only been the gift of the total European war weariness and exhaustion, not at all a reassuring reason for the absence of war. After this minimal and highly compressed but essential account of two decades of European history, he then gently makes fun of the critics who irked him by regarding his interest in war as obsessive, even pathological. "Some people used to say," he chides, "why is the man so preoccupied and obsessed with war, and now, since 1933 perhaps it is clear why a writer should be interested in the constant bullying, murderous, slovenly crime of war."

An Era of Violence and War

Thus, writing in 1949, for Hemingway nearly the whole first half of the 20th century stands accused of the "murderous, slovenly crime of war," going all the way back to the European 1908–1914 arms race, which he characteristically leaves out. What he does include is the mere mention of the virulent form of the "constant bullying" and the quasi-mystical glorification of murderous impulses in the 1933 rise of Nazi ideology. It is an ideology that regards violence as sacred within the putative prerogatives of the Aryan "master race." Hemingway might have added other bloody events he knew so much about, mainly the 1917 Bolshevik Revolution in Russia, as an armed struggle for a classless society that was to sweep away what Karl Marx and Friedrich Engels in *The Communist Manifesto* decried as "All fixed and fast-frozen [human] relations, with their train of ancient and venerable prejudices and opinions"; the surge of Italian fascism (1922) as the resurgence of the Roman Empire; and the Spanish Civil War (1936–1939). The bipolarity of these two ideologies, communism and fascism, found their common ground in totalitarian attitudes, but the Nazi and fascist ideologies appeared more inclined to acclaim unbound violence as a value in itself. Violence appeared to them to yield a panacea to individual and national powerlessness. In 1935, in "Notes on the Next War," Hemingway warns:

> In a modern war there is no Victory. The allies won the war but the regiments that marched in triumph were not the men who fought the war. The men who fought the war were dead. More than seven million of them were dead and it is the murder of over seven million more that an ex-corporal in the German army [Hitler] and an ex-aviator and former morphine addict [Mussolini] drunk with personal and military ambition and fogged in a blood-stained murk of misty patriotism look forward hysterically to today.

Hemingway's interest as a writer in all the blood-lust and bloodletting in the 20th century is also augmented by the omnipresence of their analogues throughout human history. He reminds us that "Europe has always fought, the intervals of peace are only Armistices." For him, the historical background is a melancholy reminder of our foreground, a gloomy story elaborately and intricately foretold. It is the continual preparation for and perpetual occurrence of war that force Hemingway to consider war as a subject of primary interest for a writer. Persuaded that the foretold are at least forewarned, he sounds an alarm. War, as an atavistic concern, fascinates him and compels him to reflect. He would have agreed with the Chinese warrior-philosopher Sun Tzu who holds that "Mili-

Ernest Hemingway on crutches in an American Red Cross Hospital in Milan, Italy, during World War I, circa 1918. Copyright © Corbis/AP Images.

tary action is . . . the ground of death and life, the path of survival and destruction, so it is important to examine it."

Hemingway's Complex Relation to War

However, I find no reason to suggest that war and its metaphors and metonymies heard as echoes in Hemingway's writing are in any way an advocacy of war. It is tempting to establish a connection between intellectual, literary, and personal interests and advocacy in his case, but I believe it will prove to be wading in the shallows and ultimately a spurious undertaking. It will be so regardless of the occasions for bravery and nobility, which Hemingway greatly admired, that war provides for men. There is too much evidence to the contrary. In his introduction to *Treasury for the Free World*, he is unmistakably direct about the criminality of war:

> An aggressive war is the great crime against everything good in the world. A defensive war, which must necessarily turn to aggressive at the earliest moment, is the necessary great counter-crime. But never think that war, no matter how necessary, nor how justified, is not a crime.

In "Wings [Always] Over Africa," he instructs us that "war has the essence of all of these [tyranny, injustice, murder, brutality, and the corruption of the soul] blended together and is strengthened by its various parts until it is stronger than any of the evils it is composed of can ever be." Thus he does not condone war as admissible or excusable—even though often war may be defensive, unavoidable, and inevitable. For him, as we have just seen, war always conjugates all manifestations of evil in such a way as to make them more effective in their combined demonic violence.

"War is always wrong," [German psychiatrist and philosopher] Karl Jaspers categorically proclaims—plain and simple. No casuistry of just war for Jaspers. It would seem to me Hemingway would have no quarrel with such a straightforward ethical statement. Yet, from a writer's point of view, he considers war to be a significant experience. The experience of war is consequential to him even if a writer peripherally participates in it, as Hemingway did by serving with the Red Cross on the Italian front where he was gravely wounded on July 8, 1918. Accordingly, his understanding of war—as being at once unavoidable and unacceptable, even when it places itself under the sign of counterviolence—deepens and becomes exceedingly nuanced. His fictional references to matters of war testify to the scope and complexity of his comprehension of the subject, even though his own direct war experience was limited. As an exigent life-and-death experience—a veritable *extremis* or "limit-situation," as Jasper calls it—war is no doubt for many an unsurpassable and often epiphanic experience. . . .

No to War, yet No to Slavery

Hemingway appears to have considered the concept of *jus ad bellum* or "just war" as no more than a sophistical theory at best and a mendacious one at worst. It survives to our day as the Catholic Church's desire to reconcile war and Christ's commandment, "Love thine enemies," under certain conditions or circumstances (Council of Arles 314). It was a modality of *realpolitik* which later became a part of the church's doctrine. We have already seen that Hemingway unreservedly believes war to be criminal in all its various manifestations. He finds no conditions or circumstances in which war could be sanctioned as good or legitimized as "just" as, say, [early Christian scholars] Gratian and Saint Augustine did. Correlatively, for him, the only mode of *jus in bello* or just conduct in war is to win it quickly by any means possible, regardless of who or what has initially caused it. He develops a "realistic" argument to support his negation of *jus in bello*. In his introduction to the anthology of war narrative *Men at War*, he tells us that

> The editor of this anthology, who took part and was wounded in the last war to end war [WW I], hates war and hates all the politicians whose mismanagement, gullibility, cupidity, selfishness and ambition brought on this present war [WW II] and made it inevitable. But once we have a war there is only one thing to do. It must be won. *For defeat brings worse things than any that can ever happen in a war.* (my emphasis)

For me, this paragraph makes intelligible the crux of Hemingway's thought on the conduct of war: War is irrecusably evil, always and everywhere, but worse is yet the evil of defeat. Tactically, he advises, "when the moment arrives, whether it is in a barroom fight or in a war, the thing to do is to hit your opponent the first punch and hit him as hard as possible" (*Men at War*). This statement has a Machiavellian cast to it; and yet it simply makes its way beyond expediency to another sphere of significant considerations. I discern in it Hemingway's absolute dread of defeat, which borders on a Hegelian master-slave dialectic [espoused by the German philosopher Georg Wilhelm]. Winning a war bestows the rights of the master on the winner and ushers in a period of slavery for the loser. For Hemingway, nothing less than the essence of our humanity, that is, our freedom is at stake in losing a war. The horrific upshot of losing a war makes itself manifest in the unavoidable loss of freedom and the consequent enslavement suffered by an individual, group, tribe, race, or nation. That is precisely why Hemingway can write an unthinkable sentence such as: "The answer to the Nazi claim that Germans are a superior race and other races shall be slaves is to say, and mean it, 'We will take your race and wipe it out'" (*Men at War*). And mean it? The ferocity of the sentence derives from the equally unimaginable horror of slavery for Hemingway. Thus he puts forward a subcategory of the Hegelian idea of the fight to the death, which naturally issues from the master-slave conflict, its consequent dialectic, and acquires the dimension of an imperative. Hemingway can only respond to the possibility of defeat with fury and utter contempt. A human being is always better dead than enslaved. As a consequence, he simply insists that "We must win it [this war]" (*Men at War*), which becomes for him incantatory in its necessity, intensity, and repetition.

After all is said, it is still in the name of freedom, or the negation of slavery as a mode of human existence in its totality, that he adds: "We must win it never forgetting what we are fighting for, in order that while we are fighting Fascism we do not slip into the ideas and ideals of Fascism" (*Men at War*). For fascism absolute power denies, violates, obliterates, and eventually even *surpasses* freedom as a constituent of the human condition. I would suggest that one may interpret Hemingway's startling proposal to wipe out the German race as "We will take your Nazi ideology and we will wipe it out. We mean this." In the same mode of thinking, admitting that Germans are "practical professionals in war," he counsels:

> We can learn all their lessons without being Fascists if we keep our minds open. All we need is common sense, a quality which is often conspicuously lacking in generalship but which our own Civil War produced the great masters of. We can beat the Germans without becoming Fascists. We can fight a total war without becoming totalitarians if we do not stand on our mistakes and try to cover them. . . .(*Men at War*)

On Guard Against Fascist Temptation

This passage makes sufficiently evident the radical complexity of Hemingway's metaphysics of war, which reformulates the concept of *jus ad bellum* by removing from war the possibility of enslaving the defeated. Hemingway's reference to the American Civil War in the passage becomes noteworthy in this new reformation. In his 1946 introduction to *Treasury for the Free World*, he refers to peacetime as "a more difficult time when it is a man's duty to understand his world rather than simply fight for it." He considers the understanding of one's world "to be hard work [that] will involve reading much that is unpleasant to accept. But it is one of man's first duties now." And, among other things, this unpleasant reading will make it clear to us that

> We have waged war in the most ferocious and ruthless way that it has ever been waged. We waged it against fierce and

ruthless enemies that it was necessary to destroy. . . . For the moment we are the strongest power in the world. It is very important that we do not become the most hated. (*Treasury*)

Again, Hemingway turns the fascist ideology upside down by privileging freedom over absolute power. In "On the American Dead in Spain," he writes:

The fascists may spread over the land, blasting their way with weight of metal brought from other countries. They may advance aided by traitors and by cowards. They may destroy cities and villages and try to hold people in slavery. *But you cannot hold any people in slavery.* (my emphasis)

What enslaving power seeks is temporary because freedom endures. "Just as the earth can never die, neither those who have been free return to slavery" ("American Dead"). For Hemingway, fascism is a hating, hateful, and hated ideology, in the fullest sense of those adjectives, and doomed to failure everywhere. It is also the most pernicious because it is as contagious as a plague disguised as privilege. So "we," too, can become hated to the extent that we are vulnerable to its contagion, which can easily contaminate and corrupt a "superpower." He warns that it would "be easy for us, if we do not learn to understand the world and appreciate the rights, privileges, and duties of all other countries and peoples, to represent in our power the same danger to the world that Fascism did" (*Treasury*). A terrible and terrifying possibility. He seems to agree with the ancient Taoist Chinese warrior Sun Tzu that it is best not to "celebrate victory," that "those who celebrate victory are bloodthirsty, and the bloodthirsty cannot have their way with the world." Hemingway is intensely passionate about making the conditions for a genuinely human world free from oppression a reality. He strongly admonishes that

This is no time for any nation to have any trace of the mentality of the bully. It is no time for any nation to become hated. It is no time for any nation to even swagger. Certainly it is no time for any nation to jostle. It is no time for any nation to be anything but just. (*Treasury*)

The Nobility of Heroism

As we have already seen, there exists a sufficient body of evidence in Hemingway's meditations on war to make a simple, straightforward statement: Hemingway hated war. His hatred of war, however, makes a highly intricate and multifaceted mosaic of concerns. His hatred of war should be particularly extended to the judgment he brings to men at war and those he primarily holds responsible for instigating war for ambition, venality, and sheer love of brutality. Let us begin with the judgment he renders on war profiteers. In "Wings [Always] Over Africa," he expresses the conviction that "the only people who ever loved war for long were profiteers, generals, staff officers, and whores. They all had the best and finest time of their lives and most of them made the most money they had ever made." One may assume that for him all manner of profiteering from war is a kind of whoring. It is not too difficult, however, to imagine the real whore was the most honorable, the most honest in her intention, the least harmful to others, and the least offensive to Hemingway in his roster of the whoring profiteers and professional mercenaries. Elsewhere he writes: "I believe that all the people who stand to profit by a war and who help provoke it should be shot on the first day it starts by accredited representatives of the loyal citizens of their country who will fight it." In mock seriousness, he adds he would be "very glad to be in charge of this shooting, if legally delegated by those who will fight. . . ." In these reflections, he makes a clear distinction between anyone who in any way stands to profit from the war and the combatants. It is the latter whom he sees as being "amongst the finest people that there are, or just say people, although, the closer you are to where they are fighting, the finer people you meet. . . ." It is the courage and resourcefulness, the toughness and resilience—in short, the nobility and heroism of the ordinary soldier in the face of death that he so utterly admires. The soldier becomes a veritable warrior *in extremis*, a man whose life will forever be transformed by his martial experience if he survives and conducts himself well and with grace. It is "the human heart and the human mind in war" that he finds praiseworthy and instructive (*Men at War*). The baptism of fire will either wholly engulf the warrior or shall earn him the mantle of authenticity . . . as only the warrior elite has always come to know and to incarnate. It is all a matter of combatants facing death intelligently, bravely, even exuberantly in a war not of their own making. When slain in battle, these warriors are heroes that the Norse mythology assigns to Valhalla, the paradise of heroes. It is exactly to such potential warriors that Hemingway addresses himself—if not as a former brother-in-arms at least as a participant in war and then as an older, wiser commentator. In a paragraph in *Men at War*, Hemingway offers to the book's potential World War II warrior-readers a lyrical narrative of being wounded in World War I:

> When you go to war as a boy you have a great illusion of immortality. Other people get killed; not you. It can happen to other people; but not to you. Then when you are badly wounded the first time you lose that illusion and you know it can happen to you. After being severely wounded two weeks before my nineteenth birthday I had a bad time until I figured it out that nothing could happen to me that had not happened to all men before me. Whatever I had to do men had always done. If they had done it then I could do it too and the best thing was not to worry about it.

This is a multilayered narrative of elegiac elegance and depth. The illusion of immortality partakes of a deep-running narcissism, which, incidentally, markedly influences Hemingway's writing as a whole. . . . The soldier all too quickly wakes up from this dream of immortality and has to face the verities of combat. What awaits him is the nightmarish reality of history's "killing fields" and the warrior's stoic acceptance of it and willing participation in it. As William James has put it: "Ancestral evolution has made us all potential warriors; so the most insignificant individual, when thrown into an army in the field, is weaned from whatever excess of tenderness towards his precious person he may bring with him. . . ." For both Hemingway and James, war signifies a process of divestment of narcissism, whose virulent outbursts our history has continually recorded and has mostly rationalized and glorified. It is the acceptance of war and its vicissitudes as an inextricable part of human existence that eventually dissipates the quasi-hallucinatory narcissism and gives birth to the true warrior within whose ranks Hemingway aspired to inscribe his own name.

Small Hips, Not War

Norman Friedman

Norman Friedman is an emeritus professor of English at Queens College in New York.

Many critics when reading A Farewell to Arms *have focused their attention on the significance of war and Hemingway's message on this topic within the novel. However, Norman Friedman argues in the following viewpoint that war, instead of being a focal theme on which Hemingway delivers a message, is merely a force that propels the story forward. Friedman emphasizes two main points in making this argument. First, he maintains that war is secondary to love in the majority of the books within the novel, thus proving that love is the main focus of the work. Second, he points out that any of the tragic consequences of the protagonists' love could have, and likely would have, occurred whether the novel was set in war or peacetime. Further, Friedman contends that if Hemingway had wanted to highlight the horrors of war, he would have connected Catherine's tragic end more directly to the war and not to her own biology. These factors combine, in Friedman's opinion, to create a novel in which war is merely the context in which a love story takes place.*

The pathetic misfortune which Frederic Henry suffers in losing Catherine through childbirth, at the end of *A Farewell to Arms*, is commonly interpreted as the result of one or the other of two causes, or some combination: He is seen either as the justly punished outlaw for having loved without benefit of clergy, or as the pitiful victim of the arbitrary and remorseless fortunes of war. Either way, what interests modern critics of this novel is, first, its portrait of a generation becom-

Norman Friedman, "Criticism and the Novel: Hardy, Hemingway, Crane, Woolf, Conrad," *The Antioch Review*, vol. 18, no. 3, Autumn 1958, pp. 343–370. Copyright © 1958 by The Antioch Review. All rights reserved. Reproduced by permission.

ing lost in its conflict with a middle-class industrial society which it cannot accept, and second, the way this portrait suggests the wasteland archetype in its symbolic use of rain and snow, mountain and plain, lake and river, wound and love, death in birth, and so on. Thus seen, this book is taken as making a profound artistic comment on the breakdown of values in the twentieth century: the impossibility of living and loving truly while following traditional sanctions, the consequent necessity for keeping one's guard up and taking only calculated risks, and the pathos which ensues when one of the brave is caught with his guard down.[1]

Now all of this may be true in a large and general way, but even the supporters of this interpretation have sometimes felt a sense of strain in trying to reconcile the two obviously discrete portions of the book, which their punning on its title serves to point up—the "arms" of battle and the "arms" of a woman. This is clearly, as any textbook survey will tell you, "a novel of love and war," but the relationship between the two has been taken to be largely associative and symbolic: War destroys lovers just as society destroys love, or something of the sort.

But let us see what a scrutiny of the actual events and their connections reveals. Hemingway has divided his story into five books, and the central incidents of each may be outlined as follows:

I. Henry meets Catherine, goes into battle, and is wounded.

II. He is sent to a hospital, meets her there, and their love flowers.

III. His wound is better, he goes back to the war, is caught up in a retreat, and is forced to desert.

IV. He finds his way back to Catherine, who is bearing his child.

V. They escape to neutral territory where, after some months, she dies in childbirth.

Notice first of all the proportions devoted to each of the story's two "halves": only the last part of Book I (chs. IX–XIII) and most of Book III deal with the war directly, whereas the remaining three-and-a-half books deal mainly with the love affair. This suggests that, perhaps because of Hemingway's skill in such writing, we might be overestimating the relative importance of war in the plot as a whole.

A further analysis of the causal connections among these books bears out this suggestion rather clearly. Since the main culminating incident derives its force and meaning almost entirely from the relationship between the lovers, it would not be an unreasonable hypothesis to assume that the main action of the novel is organized around that relationship. We may ask first, then, what brought about this catastrophe? And secondly, what part does the war play in this sequence?

In the first place, I think it is clear that there is one sufficient cause of Catherine's death, and one only: biology ("You always feel trapped biologically"). That is, her hips were too narrow for a normal delivery—"The doctor said I was rather narrow in the hips and it's all for the best if we keep young Catherine small"—and by the time her doctor decided a caesarian was needed, the baby had strangled itself and she had developed an internal hemorrhage.

Their love for each other, and the fact that they chose to consummate their love physically, is naturally the necessary condition for this effect. But there is no reason whatever in these circumstances as such for so terrible an outcome; nothing prevented a normal delivery except Catherine's unfortunate anatomical characteristics. The same circumstances, given wider hips, could just as easily have ended in a successful delivery; and, by the same token, the same narrowness of hips could just as easily have produced the same catastrophe in the peaceful suburbs.

They could have been married fifty times over, as Henry himself reflects, and thus the theory that he suffers for daring to defy social mores will not bear up under the weight of evidence. Similarly, he could have suffered almost as much if his love had flowered in peacetime, and thus the theory that he is a victim of the war proves equally invalid. Indeed, if we speculate as to what Hemingway could have done had he wanted to do what these theories would have him do, we will see even more clearly the lack, which they ignore, of those causal connections needed. Had Hemingway wanted to make Henry suffer for violating moral conventions, for example, he could have had Catherine's death stem directly from some mischance encountered while loving immorally—she could have contracted a venereal disease from Henry, for instance, or they could have been forced to make love under physical conditions unfavorable to normal conception, and so on. But there is absolutely no hint or implication of anything like this in the narration of the final chapters. Or again, had Hemingway wanted to make Henry suffer as a victim of the war, he could have had Catherine's death result from some contingency of battle, for which any number of gruesome possibilities suggest themselves—she could have been injured while rowing across to Switzerland, or while being caught up in the retreat, or because of having to give birth without medical attention, or under unsanitary conditions, and so on. But the fact is that she had, by and large, a quiet confinement and the best medical care and facilities available. (The possibility that it is the doctor's fault in not operating sooner presents itself, but is not supported by the text; and even if it were, would make very little sense.)

What, then, secondly, *is* the function of the war in relation to this main action? The answer may be discussed under two heads: its causal function, and its intensifying function. Causally, although the war is a sufficient condition of neither their love nor their suffering which is the outcome of this love, it does serve as a necessary condition of this love. Without it, they in all probability would never have met, and even if they had, Catherine would have still had her English fiancé. But the war, in simply bringing them together in a susceptible mood, would not in itself have thrown them in love. Indeed, Catherine met Rinaldi first without being attracted to him at all. The sufficient cause of the love between Henry and Catherine stems primarily from their respective characters and attitudes. The war, further, inflicts a wound upon Henry, which in turn allows him to see more of Catherine and thus to consummate their love; and again, by means of the retreat, the war allows him to return to her and thus to be in attendance when her time arrives. But in each case, its functional role is that of a necessary condition rather than that of a sufficient cause.

Notes

"Small Hips, Not War" (Editor's title) by Norman Friedman. From "Criticism and the Novel: Hardy, Hemingway, Crane, Woolf, Conrad," *The Antioch Review*, 17:352–55. Copyright © 1958 by Antioch Press. Reprinted by permission of Antioch Press.

1. J.W. Beach, *American Fiction 1920–1940* (New York, 1941), pp. 84 ff.; R.B. West, Jr. and R.W. Stallman, *The Art of Modern Fiction* (New York, 1952), pp. 60–66; C.H. Baker, *Hemingway: The Writer as Artist* (Princeton, 1952), Ch. V; and H.K. Russell, "The Catharsis in *A Farewell to Arms*," *MFS* [Modern Fictions Studies], I (1955), 25–30.

Death Exists in *A Farewell to Arms* to Initiate Spiritual and Physical Rebirth

Robert E. Gajdusek

Robert E. Gajdusek is a Hemingway scholar who has studied and written extensively about the author.

In the following viewpoint, Robert E. Gajdusek argues that imagery of birth and death coupled with religious symbolism combine to create the necessary context in which Frederic Henry can experience physical and spiritual rebirth in A Farewell to Arms. *Gajdusek maintains that the images of the harvest, the tunnel, and the oven each serve as a symbol of reproduction or the womb in which Frederic experiences death and, when expelled from it, is reborn. However, this expulsion and rebirth is not possible in the author's view without the assistance of paternal figures who guide the protagonist to spiritual enlightenment upon his reentry into the world. These father figures form a trinity, again borrowing from religious iconography, that Gajdusek believes ushers Frederic toward the culminating act of the ninth chapter, his baptism in blood beneath the dying man on the sling above him. Gajdusek views this cycle of birth, death, and rebirth as a central theme in Hemingway's novel.*

The ninth chapter of Ernest Hemingway's *A Farewell to Arms* is an important stage in the development of that richly structured work. In it, Hemingway establishes the symbolic and intellectual coordinates of his novel: He ventures

Robert E. Gajdusek, "The Ritualization of Death and Rebirth: The Reconstruction of Frederic Henry," *Hemingway in Italy and Other Essays*, Robert W. Lewis, ed. NY: Greenwood Publishing, 1990. Copyright © 1990 by ABC-CLIO Inc. All rights reserved. Reproduced by permission.

into death to covertly explore in ritual and myth the significance of rebirth; he studies both the process and the sexual, religious, and mythic necessities for effective psychic rebirth. . . .

In *this* chapter, where Frederic experiences death-in-life, where he undergoes death and cyclical resurrection, opposites are joined, even as they are when love is thrust into the midst of war. These oppositions, studied in dialectical opposition as well as in synthesis, prepare the reader for the antagonisms and loves of lovers and the battles and capitulations of warriors. *A Farewell to Arms* exists to force love and war together. This is partly because Hemingway was both warrior and lover. His ironic recognition, however, is that each may become its opposite: Love, that tends to bond lovers together creatively, and war that tends to oppose warriors destructively—love and war are the archetypal sources of birth and death—may invert, so that love may beget death (as it does for Catherine and Frederic) and war create birth (as it seems to in the imagery of the "pregnant" soldiers and in Frederic's multiple violent rebirths that the novel studies). . . .

Imagery of Birth and Death Set the Scene for a Heroic Adventure

In the ninth chapter, Hemingway develops a consistent imagery of birth that runs concomitantly with the facts and imagery of death. Carefully, he sets the stage for a caesarian birth, no less difficult than the one in [his short story] "Indian Camp" if more covert. His first sentence reads: "The road was crowded and there were screens of corn-stalk and straw matting on both sides and matting over the top so that it was like the entrance at a circus or a native village." Few have noted how inappropriate an imagery of circuses and aboriginal simplicity is to the front lines of battle. It is, however, necessary to Hemingway, who is establishing at the very beginning of his ninth chapter an imagery of cycles of nativity and of re-

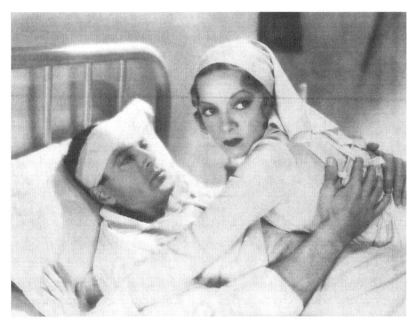

Actors Helen Hayes, as Catherine Barkley, and Gary Cooper, as Frederic Henry, embrace in a hospital bed in a scene from the 1932 screen adaptation of Hemingway's A Farewell to Arms. © Bettmann/Corbis.

turn to primitive sources. "Native" speaks of natal. The corn-stalk screens additionally speak of Demeter/Ceres [the Greek and Roman goddesses of harvest] and Persephone [Demeter's daughter], of birth and death and cyclical renewal, of seasonal fruition and the birth of crops, as well as of the death and reaping of the harvest. Hemingway lets us see that this en-trance to the place of wounding/death experience is patently a return to the womb itself. As they drive slowly down the straw matting–covered tunnel to emerge in a bare cleared space sunken below the level of the riverbank, they confront holes in the earth that are filled with infantry. These men in the holes will variously emerge to live and die, and some will die *in* them—a foreshadowing of Catherine's child's death in the womb later in the novel—and others will need assistance to be lifted from them and brought to life. The uterine journey inward down the life/death covered tunnel (made of materials that speak both of death and of life and the cycles of life and death) is one that has literary precursors, of which Hemingway could scarcely have been unaware. It is perhaps only as we reread [American novelist Herman] Melville's "Tartarus of Maids" that we discover that we are *not* being taken on a tour of a paper mill but rather on an expedition through the biology, the reproductive organs, of a woman—and *these*, indeed, *are* the Tartarus of maids. In Hemingway's biological journey, the holes in the earth where the doctors function are described as the ovens of this setting which was a brickyard. The sense of the oven as a hot source out of which emerge fully formed and created "bricks" is part of the total structure, and Hemingway twice emphasizes a distinction between the straw matting of the tunnel and the life-endorsed "obstetric" ovens from which may emerge living men restored to life. In the main "oven," Frederic notes the instruments shining in the light and the basins. This is the oven to which he must be brought after he is wounded and before he is finally delivered to the world. But before rebirth, he must first undergo wounding and death. In the wounding, he knows he is "dead," and then he feels himself "slide back." The shock of this moment is carefully described as a "blastfurnace door . . . swung open." Hemingway so describes it to suggest the trauma of a man being destroyed *or* that of an infant being expelled from the womb, and he describes it in terms that carefully and distinctly relate it to the "oven" from which he will later emerge, fully restored to life. When Frederic goes on to exclaim that it is a mistake "to think you just died," the bewildering "just" is a real clue to one major insight of the novel: birth as death, death as birth. This journey into death and back again into life is the replication in miniature of the mythic heroic journey to the other side that the true hero must make—the rebirth-return as important as the death journey in the archetype of heroic adventure.

The Father Is Associated with Rebirth

Much of the birth imagery of the chapter is associated with the feminine reproductive system of the mother, which is associated with death, darkness and disorder, but *this* imagery is annealed to a sustained parallel imagery of the father/ obstetrician role in that "delivery," which is associated with light, control, and spiritual resurrection/redemption. The two threads of imagery together produce an imagery of a doubly endorsed rebirth/restoration, one part of which is physical, the other spiritual; however, it is the spiritual resurrection which seems to save Frederic from encirclement in the womb, the fate his son suffers.

The birth/rebirth imagery takes the reader on an internal journey to the womb itself where primitive feeding occurs. It is a world of oppositions, where there are interchanges but no resolution, recognition of opposition but no definition, where passion and reason are mixed. Life in that dug-out hole is a sitting on the earth or a crouching in darkness. This point is made as a small lighter is lit and passed around by these men whose backs are most frequently described in the telling Hemingway phrase of "against the wall," but the first words said by one of the soldiers are "Why didn't we see?" Frederic, saying, "I'll go and *see* now," prepares to go back to the lighted world of the doctors he has left, and when he goes out, it is to "look" and to "see." The point is made that his men can either stay where they are *or* "look around," but sight is not a function of the cave.

It is in this almost sightless sunken hole that the men are nurtured and prepared for either life or death. There Passini dies, and from there three others emerge naturally under their own power. Frederic has to be forcibly lifted and brought out and so brought to the doctors in the light who subsequently "cut" him free and act to set him forward on his journey into the world. Hemingway uses the word "severing" to describe the doctor's action; then he writes, "The flesh was cut," and this child/man of questionable paternity is then carried toward the waiting world, undergoing a baptism of blood as he goes.

Father and Son Triumph Over Death

Hemingway carefully lets us see the intricate relationship between father and son in this victory over death and process. It is described as a spiritual victory of paternal expertise and definition over darkness and chaos in a maternal realm where dirt rains down and where multiple inversions and dissolutions are recommended. The major who is responsible for the food Frederic receives and the medical attention he is given, and who has great expectations for Frederic, is one of a group of three doctors Frederic Henry knows. To emphasize his alliance with the paternal doctor ideal, later established in Valentini, the major is given the same rank and upturned mustaches as Valentini and bears wound stripes to tell of his own successful encounters with death. It is with this trinity of doctors that Frederic first shares spirits in this lighted place amidst surrounding darkness. When he later returns to this same lighted arena to get food for his men, he finds the major sitting on a box, and it is then he sees, as the major again offers him spirits, the instruments "shining in the light" and the basin and stoppered bottles. For his men, Frederic is given pasta asciutta and cheese, pointedly retrieved from a dark hole in the back and out of sight, which he receives in a basin. This separation of the cheese/pasta from the alcohol/light is a careful separation exercised in that lighted oven/hole in the earth and speaks of the demarcations and sunderings overseen by the father figures. Later, after Frederic's wounding, after he has officiated via that basin with cheese and wine at a black mass communion offered by him as perverted priest to his men, the religious significance that Hemingway has been developing about the trinity of doctors with their implements, vaguely suggesting a mass to sustain the spirit as well as an operation to save/restore the body, is established.

The Paternal Trinity of Role Models After Rebirth

After Frederic is wounded, he is unable to move, and so he must be lifted out: "Some one took hold of me under the arms and somebody else lifted my legs." Before he is lifted, he notes that a trinity has survived: that the explosion that almost meant his death has effectively removed from him the contaminating fourth, Passini: "That left three." Being carried to the oven where three doctors await, he is twice dropped. The imagery of his wounding is that of death/resurrection, and that of his lifting is the classical imagery of Christ's descent from the cross. The subsequent falls on the journey to the oven suggest the stages of the cross on Calvary. That this imagery seems reversed should not trouble a critic who has studied similarly frequent ironic inversions of religious ritual in *The Sun Also Rises, Green Hills of Africa*, and "A Clean, Well-Lighted Place." Such inversion is central to Hemingway's statement: Frederic is, after all, coming back to life through a sort of rebirth and not being brought to heaven through death.

The spiritual/obstetric part of the process of spiritual/ physical rebirth takes place at the main oven, formerly dominated by the three spirit-giving doctors. Here the question of paternity is the first question raised. First Frederic is called the legitimate son of President Wilson, and then he is described as "the only son of the American Ambassador." At this frontline aid station, he now confronts a *new* trinity of totally admirable paternal role models. Later, the reader will see Frederic in Milan confronting three inadequate nurses (mother figures), then three rear-echelon impotent ineffective false doctors (surrogate fathers)—all before Valentini arrives to look after him. Now, at the ovens, the first male of three who take charge of Frederic is the tall British driver who has arrived there with three ambulances. He is active, effective, concerned, and spirited. He steps carefully among the wounded, speaks perfect Italian, bypasses procedure and protocol by seizing control of events, and establishes Frederic's fictional paternity to give him special status and attention, as he also anticipates Frederic's subsequent needs. Next, the little Italian major oversees the operating room, readily speaks French, and shows resilience, as he accommodates the driver's rearranged priorities, and active control, as he continues to operate on others while accepting Frederic. A third officer takes Frederic on his operating table. As he dictates and talks while investigating, probing, injecting and cutting Frederic, he demonstrates the easy reconciliation of humanity and expertise, efficiency and humor, objective curiosity and concern, speed and accuracy, that mark the humanity of the Hemingway hero: His hands move "fast," his bandages come "taut and sure." He offers brandy (spirits) to Frederic, has a cross put on both Frederic's legs, and to him Frederic offers his three exclamations, "Christ, yes!" and, twice, "Good Christ!"

It is part of Hemingway's sustained iconography that as Frederic emerges from under the care/concern of these three "fathers," he comes out to have the sergeant-adjutant kneel down "beside me where I lay." The chapter ends as he is baptized by the stream of blood that falls upon him from above, from the man who dies above him in the slings.

"Going All to Pieces": A Farewell to Arms as Trauma Narrative

Trevor Dodman

Trevor Dodman is a literary scholar who serves as an assistant professor of English at Hood College.

In the following viewpoint, Dodman describes A Farewell to Arms *as a trauma narrative in which Frederic Henry continually revisits wounds and losses as he recounts in the present the events of his wartime experiences. According to Dodman, Frederic's attempt to retell the past is a prosthetic device he hopes might bring healing and understanding to his psychic and physical wounds. However, the trauma associated with his injury and the loss of his beloved Catherine is inexplicable. Unable to suture these gaping wounds that persist in his postwar life, Frederic is compelled to mentally reexperience them in a doomed effort to find closure.*

Bullet wounds do not cause severe bleeding unless they happen to injure some large trunk or smash one of the larger bones. Wounds caused by fragments of shells or bombs tear larger holes in the skin and lacerate the muscles and are, therefore, more often the cause of serious bleeding.—*Injuries and Diseases of War* (15)

In the final chapter of *A Farewell to Arms*, the narrator and main character, Frederic Henry, describes the protracted labor of his partner, Catherine Barkley. When the attending physician recommends a caesarian section, Frederic anxiously inquires about the dangers associated with the procedure. As-

Trevor Dodman, "'Going All to Pieces': *A Farewell to Arms* as Trauma Narrative," *Twentieth Century Literature*, vol. 53, no. 3, Fall 2006, pp. 249–274. Copyright © 2006 by Twentieth Century Literature. All rights reserved. Reproduced by permission.

suring him that the risks should not exceed those associated with an "ordinary delivery," the doctor responds to Frederic's question regarding the potential aftereffects of the operation: "There are none. There is only the scar" (321). Although this reply suggests that what remains will be of no lingering concern, *A Farewell to Arms* nonetheless testifies to the persistence of wounds, both visible and invisible. Frederic's particular narration of the events and experiences that mark his wartime years must be understood in such terms, for his entire narrative—no "ordinary delivery"—inscribes a continued struggle with the debilitating aftereffects associated with shell shock. He suffers from the compulsion to remember and retell his traumatic past from the standpoint of a survivor both unable and perhaps unwilling to put that very past into words; the novel stands as a record of his narrative collision with the violence of trauma.[1]

Frederic's troubled recollections find expression in apparently embodied and disembodied ways: as pain that registers at the level of the body, breaking apart the perceived unity of the physical self in the presence of terrific bodily suffering; and as trauma that registers at the level of consciousness, breaking down time, language, and the perceived unity of the subjective self in the face of incomprehensible violence. However, in staging an ongoing dialogue between inside and outside, *A Farewell to Arms* also challenges us to reconsider the mind/body dualism that keeps the wounds of the body separate from the wounds of the mind. For Frederic's narration—of his body, his memory, his wounds—destabilizes such distinctions in an effort to hold together a broken past that remains, in the present, a nexus of uncertainty and contestation. In accord with Tim Armstrong's emphasis on the interpenetration of machine and human in the modernist period, and with his identification of the "prosthetic thinking" (3) involved in the repair and augmentation of bodies in the face of radical disruption in warfare, Frederic's narration enacts a kind of prosthetic thinking: He repairs and augments his past as a countermeasure for the pain and trauma that plague him still.[2]

Looking back on events, reconstructing his memories, Frederic reveals a desire for a whole and perfect retelling of the past; his narration functions as a prosthesis meant to stave off a sense of the self as a disarticulated scar. His embodied subjectivity, like the wounds he suffers to represent, calls out for prosthetic completion. But as Elaine Scarry notes, "what is remembered in the body is well remembered" (112), and Frederic's narrative prosthesis cannot hold the wound closed. His traumatic memories bleed into and disrupt his present; his narration operates both as scar and wound, as tissue stitched together and lacerated apart. Though his prosthetic version of events insists on the potential for a "separate peace," Frederic's telling of his past instead goes "all to pieces" (322) in the enduring presence of pain and trauma too "well remembered" to be left behind.

For years, analysts of the novel understood that Hemingway himself was doing the remembering—the author recalling his Great War experiences through his cipher, Frederic Henry.[3] While it seems to me simply impossible to imagine anyone's being wounded in war and not having it affect his or her writing of a novel about war memories and characters who are wounded, I am not principally interested in either the text or the trauma of Hemingway's life but rather in the text of his narrator's trauma. For Frederic's narrative, I contend, unfolds in keeping with the work of prominent trauma theorists such as Dominick LaCapra, who describes trauma as a "disruptive experience that disarticulates the self and creates holes in existence; it has belated effects that are controlled only with difficulty and perhaps never fully mastered" (41).[4] In Frederic's case, the disarticulation of the self occurs in a narrative that shifts unpredictably between past and present, between the time of the action and the time of the telling. To reconstruct the past he must confront the "holes" in his subjective experience of the war, despite the fact that he might not have full mastery over the memories.

Although accounts of the novel often emphasize the centrality of memory in analyzing Frederic's narration, critics have not fully pursued the implications of the fact that the narrative consciousness in charge of these memories is one that has been traumatized.[5] Diane Price Herndl touches on the novel's traumatic terrain, briefly discussing Frederic in the context of shell shock before going on to argue that his "illness" is "masculinity as it was presented to the World War I soldier" (39). While Herndl assesses the silencing of Frederic in terms of sociocultural technologies of the male self, I find in the novel's "enforced silences" the disruptive workings of traumatic memories aggressively imposing themselves on the survivor.[6] Indeed, Frederic's particular narrative "survival" demands extra attention in light of the key critical tendency to focus on the extent to which Frederic changes over the course of the novel. According to James Phelan, Frederic begins the novel as a "naive narrator but also as a character who does not understand the war or the larger destruction of the world" (56); in Michael Reynolds's view, Frederic is a "changed man" ("Doctors" 119) after his wounding. Phelan and Reynolds read in the novel a diminishing ironic gap between the time of the action and the time of the telling, and a corresponding closing of moral distance between Frederic the character and Frederic the narrator. In contrast, I suggest that *A Farewell to Arms* warrants consideration as a trauma narrative that enacts the collapsing of such distinctions.[7] From the very first page of the novel Frederic suffers from shell shock; his voice is always already the voice of a traumatized survivor of grievous wounds and losses. A "changed man" from the outset, his narrative reveals the continued and unchanging hold that his painful past has on his present. My argument, in short, rests on the belief that all of *A Farewell to Arms* must be considered in terms of traumatic aftereffects.

Horrified participant and helpless witness, Frederic, along with his traumatic exposure to dismemberment, killing, and death comes to us via the mediation of his own narration. As Joanna Bourke reminds us,

> there is no "experience" independent of the ordering mechanisms of grammar, plot, and genre, and this is never more the case than when attempting to "speak" the ultimate transgression—killing another human being. (358)

The heuristic imperatives built into "speaking" about trauma add social dimensions to subjective and interior processes. In Kirby Farrell's terms, trauma remains a "psychocultural" matter, an injury that "demands to be interpreted and, if possible, integrated into character." Frederic's narrative task, then, is always double: He must tell the story of his shell-shocked past, integrate it into his "character" (7), while at the same time confronting the shell shock in his present as it transgresses on his capacity to tell. The retrospective organization of his traumatic experiences reflects the simultaneity of his now and then, or as James Young puts matters, the

> survivor's memory includes both experiences of history and of memory, the ways memory has already become part of personal history, the ways misapprehension of events and the silences that come with incomprehension were parts of events as they unfolded then *and* part of memory as it unfolds now. (280)

Frederic's past intrudes on his present, and his interpretation of his injury takes shape in his prosthetic reconstitution of painful and traumatic events and experiences.[8] Bodies bleed in this novel, at times uncontrollably, and Frederic's narrative likewise suffers at times from troubling and uncontrollable outflow. Frederic's prosthetic interventions, his efforts at control, underscore collapsing distinctions between the artificial and the natural, between the mind and the body, and between the past and the present. Prosthetics challenge such distinctions by explicitly drawing our attention to relations of difference. For David Wills, prosthetic relations not only complicate the perceived relation of animate and inanimate but also, at the same time, insist on the measured distance between such domains. The prosthetic emerges in the "articulation of two heterogeneities" (30) but also in the very gap that opens up between a truncated limb and its mechanical extension. As Wills writes:

> no amputation is performed without the forethought of a workable prosthesis; the knife doesn't strike indiscriminately but is guided by the range of prostheses that wait, parasitic, for a suitable host. In this respect the prosthetic possibility determines the shape of the human, the artificial determines the form of the natural. (29)

In the context of *A Farewell to Arms*, Frederic jokes with his doctors about his desire to have his knee cut off, so that he can "wear a hook on it" (97). While Frederic's sarcasm here comments on the incompetence of these particular doctors, his narration itself takes shape as a "workable prosthesis," a hook worn in the place of a lost limb, in spite of—rather than as a result of—the fact that his pain, his wounding, his losses, his trauma do "strike indiscriminately." That is, his narration must confront a traumatic rupturing of the self that cannot be prepared for ahead of time.

In the case of his own wounding, Frederic describes the experience of being hit with shell fragments in a prominent stream-of-consciousness passage:

> I tried to breathe but my breath would not come and I felt myself rush bodily out of myself and out and out and out and all the time bodily in the wind. I went out swiftly, all of myself, and I knew I was dead and that it had all been a mistake to think you just died. Then I floated, and instead of going on I felt myself slide back. I breathed and I was back. (54)

American actor Rock Hudson portrays a wounded Frederic Henry being escorted by medics in the 1957 screen adaptation of Hemingway's A Farewell to Arms. © Interfoto / Alamy.

Here Frederic describes a feeling of breaching as he rushes out of himself, his as-yet unnamed, unarticulated wounds producing an exchange across the membrane of the self. His perceptions of his wounding experience emphasize the passivity and helplessness of his situation: He can't control his breathing, he convulses outward and then floats inward at the behest of unknown and unalterable forces; he mistakes the experience as a whole for the certainty of death only to make a gentle return to the uncertainties of life.[9]

Testifying to the profound destabilizations that accompany the passive witnessing of the body's disruption, Frederic registers here a paradoxical and confusing disarticulation of the self into selves: "I felt myself rush bodily out of myself. ... I felt myself slide back." Bessel A. van der Kolk and Onno van der Hart describe the feeling of uncoupling that Frederic experiences here: "Many trauma survivors report that they automatically are removed from the scene; they look at it from a distance or disappear altogether, leaving other parts of their personality to suffer and store the overwhelming experience" (168). Floating outward, Frederic experiences his wounding at a remove: He rushes out of his wounded body and then glides back into its consolidating confines. Importantly, he also looks at it "from a distance" to the extent that his version of the wounding comes at a considerable temporal remove. His "watching" of the events takes shape in his narration of them, and his return therefore not only describes the recoupling of self and body in the time of the action but also functions as a simultaneous reexperiencing at the time of the telling. Frederic's narration not only describes a past dissociative event but becomes in itself, in its very telling, a terribly present dissociative event.[10] Experienced in the moment of the explosion as a terrifying shuttling back and forth across breached boundaries, his wounding offers, in its recounting, a record of an uncontrollable reexperiencing of the events—a collapsing of distance between past and present. Thus, in the same way that he at once feels both inside of and outside of his "self," he feels himself "slide back" to the moment of his wounding in the moment of his telling.

While the content of such a passage certainly marks his overt efforts to describe in detail the traumatic events suffered, the desperate tone hints at the frustration Frederic feels as he attempts to describe what he cannot forget but cannot manage to put into words. In fact, he quickly resorts to shocking understatement to try to relate events: "I knew that I was hit and leaned over and put my hand on my knee. My knee wasn't there. My hand went in and my knee was down on my shin" (55). The effect is jarring as the vague "out and out and out" crashes into the specific horror of "my knee was down on my shin." Frederic's disembodied sense of floating, his peaceful calm, his relief as he feels himself return to his body—"I was back"—all of these experiences explode apart with the sudden understanding that the perceived integrity of his body has been radically disrupted. The momentary return to wholeness he narrates is important, for it reveals prosthetic thinking that seeks to keep the body together; however, this unity lasts but a short interval before being shattered by the insistence of the body's "well-remembered" wounds.

Reconstructing the scene of his own reconstruction, Frederic again grapples with dissociative aftereffects. Though the medical sergeant who wraps up his damaged legs notes that "there was so much dirt blown into the wound that there had not been much hemorrhage" (57), Frederic's condition still demands immediate intervention in a battlefield dressing station. While the doctor probes for shell fragments in his legs and wraps up Frederic's fractured skull, Frederic lies helpless and in pain on the "hard and slippery" operating table, surrounded by "chemical smells and the sweet smell of blood" (59). Frederic recalls a conversation and operation occurring simultaneously:

The medical captain, "What hit you?"

Me, with eyes shut, "A trench mortar shell."

The captain, doing things that hurt sharply and severing tissue—"Are you sure?"

Me—trying to lie still and feeling my stomach flutter when
the flesh was cut, "I think so."

Captain doctor—(interested in something he was finding),
"Fragments of enemy trench-mortar shell. Now I'll probe
for some of this if you like but it's not necessary. I'll paint
all of this and—Does that sting? Good, that's nothing to
how it will feel later. The pain hasn't started yet." (59)

The simultaneity of probing and talking about it provides an
analogue for the dissociative elements governing a recollection
that operates as both a retelling and a reliving of a painful reality. Like the doctor who insists that probing the wound is
"not necessary" but does so anyway, Frederic's restaging here
suggests that his probing of the past simply cannot be avoided,
no matter how sharply it hurts. Though he tries to "lie still,"
tries to establish a protective prosthetic distance between a
"Me" who experiences and an "I" who remembers, these self-
articulations bleed together in the face of the extremities involved. The pain that arises on the operating table with the
probing of a wound brings to Frederic the pain experienced in
the moment of his wounding: The "Me" on the table shoots
"out and out and out" and back into the "I" of the explosion.
Likewise, a dynamic of deferred immediacy marks Frederic's
narration of the operation: The "I" looking back at the "Me"
on the table brings a chronic condition into contact with its
acute origins.

Despite a subsequent series of operations and other treatments, all designed to allow for his return to the front,
Frederic's knee does not make a full recovery. Rinaldi runs his
finger along the scar and painfully tests the range of motion:
"It's a crime to send you back. They ought to get complete articulation" (166). Just as the exigencies of the war call for
Frederic's return to duty with a still-damaged knee, so too
does his narration compulsively return to the operations in-

volved with a partially articulated sense of the past. Well aware that in many respects the "pain hasn't started yet," his recollection of various procedures consistently reveals the prosthetic thinking at work in their management. At one point, for instance, Frederic's wounded legs must be X-rayed, a process "arranged by holding up the shoulders, that the patient should see personally some of the larger foreign bodies through the machine" (94). Although Frederic himself earlier refers to these items as "old screws and bedsprings and things" (85), the doctor attending to his X-rays has a decidedly more serious opinion of the matter: "He declared that the foreign bodies were ugly, nasty, brutal. The Austrians were sons of bitches" (94).

Frederic confronts here, at a remove and via the "eyes" of a machine, his own disrupted, penetrated body—a body "invaded" by metal Austrians out on maneuver quite literally inside enemy territory. Thus, while he must confront the terrible bodily consequences of modern warfare, he also faces a decidedly modern paradox, as his own experience of bodily integrity—disrupted both by the metal fragments and the X-rays that locate them—depends on continued technological intervention. Frederic's survival depends on seeing the foreign bodies "through the machine," a move that places his felt experience of his wounding's painful reality in a subsidiary relation to that of a machine-produced vision of the causes of the wounds. Full of holes, Frederic's body can only be reconstituted through the mediation of a mechanical device. His experience with the X-rays reveals precisely how modernity, in Armstrong's terms, "brings both a fragmentation and augmentation of the body in relation to technology; it offers the body as lack, at the same time as it offers technological compensation" (3).

The gap that opens up between lack and compensation, between Frederic's disrupted body and his body-made-whole by machine intervention, emerges in the text as Frederic refers to himself in the third person as the "patient" (94). Echoing the earlier dissociation of "Me" and "I," Frederic employs a similar prosthesis as a way for him to imagine and represent not his own imperfect, nonstandard body but rather the body of another, the body of a perfectly standard patient. His act of divesting himself of the patient that he was also carries with it a corresponding disregard for the patient that he remains. Recourse to such reconstructive surgery, however, while speaking to a desire for prosthetic wholeness, also underscores the notion that desired-for wholeness is as much a construct as any generalized concept of patient.

The disjunction between the wounded Frederic and the "patient," articulated as an uncanny interpenetration of body and machine, reminds us that the human body is, according to Lennard J. Davis, "always already a fragmented body" (62).[11] Frederic establishes here a prosthetic relation to the "patient" as a means of bypassing the awareness of his own body as a fragmented, penetrated disunity: that body seen through the X-ray machine is not "mine" but merely the body of the "patient." He disarticulates himself from his own fragmented body, an act that prefigures later divestments of the body, such as when Frederic insists that his reconstructed knee belongs not to himself but to the doctor who performed the operation: "It was his knee all right. The other knee was mine. Doctors did things to you and then it was not your body any more" (231). In the first instance, Frederic distances himself from his own fragmented status as a patient and reveals a desire for a continued understanding of the self as a whole. In the second, though he foregrounds his fragmentation—*that* knee is *his*—he simultaneously reveals a continued experience of the wounded body as a site of control and order, a place where parts must still be understood as possessions of a whole self that survives: *This* knee is *mine*.

And yet, just as the line between a patient and his prosthesis inevitably blurs, just as the border between past and present dissolves, so too do certainties over bodily possession—over the integrity of the self—come undone in the face of extreme experiences and in the memories of those experiences. If, as Scarry concludes, "the record of war survives in the bodies, both alive and buried, of those who were hurt there" (113), then Frederic's narrative testifies to this. It records the story of his body's hurting and his body's survival, but buried in this record too are the remains of other bodies hurt beyond repair: Aymo, a shot sergeant, a stillborn son, Catherine. His wounding and the wounding of others leave their trace on the narrative in the form of prosthetic measures meant to keep their particular losses at bay. At the same time though, like a local anaesthetic "which froze the tissue and avoided pain until the probe, the scalpel or the forceps got below the frozen portion" (94), Frederic's prosthesis cannot mitigate the overwhelming losses. He may want to make things whole, but he cannot evade the trauma.

> The principles of the treatment of haemorrhage are well established, and are the same for both civil and military practice, and these principles lay down an essential rule that bleeding is to be arrested by pressure upon, or ligature of, the bleeding point itself, and not by constriction of the limb above or by tying the artery on the proximal side of the injury.—*Injuries and Diseases of War* (15)

After his initial operation, Frederic is sent to a field hospital farther behind the lines. On the journey, the man above him, suffering an unstoppable hemorrhage, bleeds onto the immobile Frederic. For a while, he notes, the "stream kept on," but eventually the drops of blood "fell very slowly, as they fall from an icicle after the sun has gone" (61). Soon he feels the man's blood pooling up around his own body: "Where it had run down under my shirt it was warm and sticky." *A Farewell to Arms* sketches a brief history of this man's bleeding to death, but it also stands as a record of that which sticks to Frederic's recounting of his own troubled past. If history, as

Cathy Caruth contends, "is precisely the way we are implicated in each other's traumas" (*Unclaimed* 24), then Frederic remains implicated in the trauma of the man above him as he collects the blood that drains out of him and collects it again as he narrates the events in the present. The stream keeps on. At the same time, however, as LaCapra notes,

> certain wounds, both personal and historical, cannot simply heal without leaving scars or residues in the present; there may even be a sense in which they have to remain as open wounds even if one strives to counteract their tendency to swallow all of existence and incapacitate one as an agent in the present. (144)

Frederic's prosthetic efforts to "counteract" the memories of passively collecting another man's blood, to arrest the hemorrhaging of his past into his present, stand also as a reckoning with the continued activity of trauma's open wounds. Just as Frederic suspects that wars "weren't won anymore," his narrative expresses anxieties about the uncontrollable persistence of traumatic memories: "Maybe they went on forever" (118).

According to van der Kolk and van der Hart, extreme encounters disrupt the ordinary processing and integrating of experience into narrative memory. Unable to assimilate such disturbing events, the survivor visits the traumatic memories again and again, tends to his or her open wounds, in an involuntary effort to attach meaning to the horrors. Many survivors, they write, "experience long periods of time in which they live, as it were, in two different worlds: the realm of the trauma and the realm of their current, ordinary life"—and it is very often "impossible to bridge these two worlds" (163). Like the prosthetic thinking that governs Frederic's dissociated relations to the "Me" and the "I" of his wounding, to the "patient" he was and continues to be, so too do the novel's many stream-of-consciousness passages operate as instances of efforts to articulate past wounds in a "current, ordinary life" of continued suffering. Early in the novel, Frederic's drunken discussion with the priest puts into circulation a number of elements that his narrative continually returns to: "I tried to tell about the night and the difference between the night and the day and how the night was better unless the day was very clean and cold and I could not tell it; as I cannot tell it now" (13). Although Frederic's narration here precedes the revelation that he suffered a serious wound, it nevertheless disrupts chronology and thereby foregrounds his enduring commitment to an experience that continually defies his efforts to narrate it. Despite his losses, he feels compelled to try again to tell the story, but finds that time has not helped him represent his experience. "I cannot tell it now": the admission speaks to his struggle to articulate a set of wartime experiences that remain resistant to the meaning-making structures of language.

The comment echoes later, when Catherine asks Frederic to explain the retreat from Caporetto. "I'll tell you about it if I ever get it straight in my head," he replies (250). But despite his repeated claims that he cannot tell his trauma, cannot put the story together for others or for himself, he does make revealing efforts to find a language for his experiences. Remembering his reunion with Catherine after his escape from the army, Frederic cycles back to his earlier remarks to the priest, blending past and present:

> We could feel alone when we were together, alone against the others. It has only happened to me like that once. I have been alone while I was with many girls and that is the way you can be most lonely. But we were never lonely and never afraid when we were together. I know the night is not the same as the day: that all things are different, that the things of the night cannot be explained in the day, because they do not then exist, and the night can be a dreadful time for lonely people once their loneliness has started. (249)

Infusing this passage is Frederic's continued awareness that Catherine's permanent absence gives lasting shape to any articulation of the loneliness of the night. On the train to

Mestre, her absence shapes his description—there's a "hard floor for a wife"—and he thinks to himself, "you loved some one else whom now you knew was not even to be pretended there" (232). He now knows that what happened to him "once" is not a singularity closed off in the past but rather a complex of ongoing physiological and psychological disturbances in his present.

Frederic's attempts to articulate the "things of the night" repeatedly involve his hospitalization and link his wound with the loss of Catherine. Considering his always already traumatized state of mind, the following scene—describing a fantasy, before he is wounded, of his first night alone with Catherine—is particularly telling for its complex deployment of prosthetic thinking:

> After supper I would go and see Catherine Barkley. I wish she were here now. I wished I were in Milan with her. I would like to eat at the Cova and then walk down Via Manzoni in the hot evening and cross over and turn off along the canal and go to the hotel with Catherine Barkley. Maybe she would. Maybe she would pretend that I was her boy that was killed and we would go in the front door and the porter would take off his cap and I would stop at the concierge's desk and ask for the key and she would stand by the elevator and then we would get in the elevator and it would go up very slowly clicking at all the floors and then our floor and the boy would open the door and stand there and she would step out and I would step out and we would walk down the hall and I would put the key in the door and open it and go in and then take down the telephone and ask them to send a bottle of capri bianca in a silver bucket full of ice and you would hear the ice against the pail coming down the corridor and the boy would knock and I would say leave it outside the door please. (37–38)

Several revealing moments emerge, not the least of which is the sudden intrusion of the present—"I wish she were here now"—on a recollection that documents his past desires, suggesting Frederic's existence in "two worlds," the ordinary and the traumatic. Departing briefly from the narrative lines along which ordinary memory runs, Frederic's traumatic memory registers itself here, out of time and ahead of itself. His story of this vision in the past simultaneously registers his hopeless desire for Catherine in the present.

Of greater interest, however, is how the rest of the novel gradually reveals the extent to which prosthetic thinking controls this entire passage. For this fantasy is nothing less than an idealized, prosthetically perfect vision of a series of experiences that, as it emerges later, are structured by Frederic's wound. The fantasy amalgamates and sterilizes—cleans out— three future episodes, performing a pastiche of wholeness, a radical effacing of Frederic's disrupted self. For in fact, Frederic and Catherine sleep together for the first time not in a Milan hotel after a romantic dinner but in a Milan hospital before breakfast is served. He does not arrive there with her after a pleasant walk along the canal but travels from the "freight yard" (81) to the hospital in an ambulance. There is no concierge desk, no boy to open the elevator door, and he rides the elevator not with Catherine but with two stretcher-bearers who ignominiously bend his legs to fit into the crowded space. He and Catherine do not walk along the hall together, and there is no key to put in the door; instead, Frederic feels the pain "going in and out of the bone" (83) as they carry him down a long hallway before putting him to bed.

A later episode is likewise prostheticized by the hotel fantasy:

At the door of the hospital the porter came out to help with the crutches. I paid the driver, and then we rode upstairs in the elevator. Catherine got off at the lower floor where the nurses lived and I went on up and went down the hall on my crutches to my room. (113)

Again, he and Catherine do not walk to a hotel and have the porter bring them up a bottle of wine; instead, they return to the hospital where a porter helps with the crutches, a crucial sign of Frederic's disrupted body. Furthermore, they find themselves separated on entering the hospital—their liaison punctuated at every turn by the realities of hospital life, by her role as a nurse and by the limits of his status as an invalid. Where Frederic once wishes for a silver bucket of ice left outside the door, he finds himself now crutching along the corridors of the hospital after Catherine, a nurse's aide carrying the "basins" (113) of the other patients.

Of course, the couple at last do walk along the canal, share a hotel room in Milan, hear the clicking of the elevator as it goes up to their floor, enjoy a bottle of Capri together. However, the experience is anything but idyllic. In light of his imminent return to the front, they are both despondent. Though the purchase of a new pistol, ironically enough, brightens the mood, they arrive at the hotel only to find it worn and disreputable. "This was the best hotel we could get in," Frederic notes, and the blend of red plush furnishings and satin bedding in their many-mirrored room leave Catherine feeling "like a whore" (152). Though they do manage to enjoy themselves—"After we had eaten we felt fine, and then after, we felt very happy" (153)—they nonetheless spend the remainder of their little time together discussing the logistics of their expected child, and joking apprehensively about the possibility of Frederic being wounded again. Their time together is marked by shame, tension, and uncertainty—hardly the "whole night" that the prosthetic version seamlessly delivers.

Frederic's fantasy thus is governed by a powerful measure of prosthetic thinking meant to stave off the painful awareness not only of his wounding and subsequent hospital treatments but also of other losses. Crucially, like the field service postcard he sends home with everything crossed out except "I am well" (36), Frederic's prosthetic fantasy involves "crossing out"

Catherine's loss. Wishing she were here now, wishing he was still "with the British" (37), he disregards not only the fact of Catherine's death at the end of the novel but also that she's been "gone" from its very beginning. Just as in his dream she insists "This doesn't make any difference between us. . . . I'm always here. I come whenever you want me" (198), Frederic disregards distance and death as he reconstitutes Catherine in his present. "Always here," she is essential to his efforts to re-constitute himself in the context of her ongoing absence; nar-rating his present into wholeness requires that Catherine's broken past emerge here intact and filled once again with po-tential: "That was how it ought to be" (38). Casting himself in the role of a fiancé blown to bits, Frederic fantasizes about his capacity to compensate for Catherine's loss: "Maybe she would. Maybe she would pretend that I was her boy that was killed" (37). The reiteration emphasizes, however, the capacity of traumatic experiences to break apart any provisional efforts at pretending away the lingering pain. The awkward wording also reflects the inevitability of trauma's return as Catherine once more confronts the loss of "her boy that was killed." That that return should implicate Frederic seems fitting, more-over, given his own continuing trauma. For in fact, though he figures himself here as the embodiment of Catherine's loss, such make-believe—even in the context of a fantasy—cannot prevent the loss of Catherine from continuing to embody him.

> If bleeding has been difficult to stop, a note should always be made on the field medical card, and this should also be marked "Urgent," in large letters.—*Injuries and Diseases of War* (17)

Just as his wounding breaches his perception of the bound-aries of the embodied subject, so too does bearing witness to Catherine's death destabilize the boundaries between Frederic and his partner. "We're the same one" (299), he once tells her, and, like a scar, she stubbornly remains, her losses and wounds incorporated as his own: "The head was mine, and the inside of the belly" (231). Elizabeth Grosz argues that scars become "loci of exchange between the inside and the outside, points of conversion of the outside into the body, and of the inside out of the body" (36). But as points of conversion, as neither inside nor outside, scars and, worse yet, open wounds challenge the limits of both representation and empathetic response. In Frederic's case, Catherine's cesarean section and hemorrhaging death demand his witness, both then and now. Her loss becomes a destabilizing point of conversion between his past and present. Difficult to stop, too "well remembered" to be countered by prosthetic thinking, Catherine's loss, her echoing voice and broken body, takes shape as a trauma narrative relentlessly imposing itself on Frederic's ordinary narrative progression of events.

Paul Fussell described the shocking horrors of mechanized mass slaughter in related terms: "the Great War was perhaps the last to be conceived as taking place within a seamless, purposeful 'history' involving a coherent stream of time running from past through present to future" (21). More recently, Trudi Tate considers veterans and civilians alike struggling to convey a "history one has lived through but not seen, or seen only partially" (1). Thus, in the place of a coherent stream of time, trauma survivors experience what Caruth describes as a future and past united "through a profound discontinuity" (*Unclaimed* 14). In Frederic's narrative, this shattering of his subjective experience of time, this radical discontinuity between his traumatic history and traumatized present, is repeatedly figured by references to the breaking of individuals, epitomized by Catherine's cry "I'm going all to pieces" (322). In elaborating this—"I'm not brave anymore, darling. I'm all broken. They've broken me. I know it now" (323)—Catherine gives voice to a whole set of concerns about the disunity of the embodied subject, confirming what Frederic already knows about himself: that "the legs"—his own legs—resemble "freshly ground hamburger steak" (95).

If we return, then, to their first night at the hotel after he deserts, we find Frederic speaking Catherine's later words: "The world breaks every one and afterward many are strong at the broken places. But those it will not break it kills. It kills the very good and the very gentle and the very brave impartially" (249). Her words, that is, appear as a traumatic intrusion of the past on a retrospective narrative given in the present. Like an echo before the sound, like the "sudden interiors of houses" (6) that appear to Frederic after bouts of shelling, these words register in the text disconcertingly out of place and ahead of their time. Fulfilling what Caruth identifies as the traumatic potential for "the outside [to go] inside without any mediation," they become Frederic's words; he gives them voice—or rather they voice themselves through him, illustrating how "the experience of a trauma repeats itself, exactly and unremittingly, through the unknowing acts of the survivor and against his very will" (2).

Catherine's feeling that she is "going all to pieces" becomes literalized on the operating table, raising the question once more of the relation of a body in pain to a traumatized mind:

> I thought Catherine was dead. She looked dead. Her face was gray, the part of it that I could see. Down below, under the light, the doctor was sewing up the great long, forcep-spread, thick-edged, wound. Another doctor in a mask gave the anaesthetic. Two nurses in masks handed things. It looked like a drawing of the Inquisition. I knew as I watched I could have watched it all, but I was glad I hadn't. I do not think I could have watched them cut, but I watched the wound closed into a high welted ridge with quick skilful-looking stitches like a cobbler's, and was glad. When the wound was closed I went out into the hall and walked up and down again. (325)

Broken apart and sewn back together, Catherine takes center stage in the operating theater. However, as the wound gets closed she seems to get swallowed up by it, disappearing from the scene, becoming, in effect, all wound. Frederic no longer sees Catherine anesthetized on the table but only the wound: great, long, forcep-spread, thick-edged, high-welted, closed. Her reduction to an unspeaking wound would seem to contrast with Frederic's position, both as a witness in the gallery and as the narrator of the scene. At the same time, however, the moment replays Frederic's own wounding and battlefield operation. He thinks she's dead, just as he once "knew" he had died; he looks down from above on Catherine's body, just as he once floated out from his own; he avoids watching the "cutting," just as he does while on the slippery table himself. Catherine's disrupted, broken body thus confronts him with his own shattered frame; her unknowing, passive silence confronts him with the wordless holes in his own experience.

Overwhelmed, Frederic shifts suddenly to relate the parable of the ants. The detail and specificity of the memory—the ants scurrying back and forth on the burning log, his steaming rather than saving them (327)—contrast with the vagueness of its time and place. Does it happen before the war, or after? Before Catherine's death, or in the aftermath? Either way, witnessing Catherine's cesarean section and death, Frederic turns to a time and place where a sense of his own agency, however ambivalent, remains intact. The respite, however, is only momentary, and Frederic returns to the scene of the wounds that won't heal: "So now I sat out in the hall and waited to hear how Catherine was" (328). From Frederic's double perspective at the time of the telling Catherine is, of course, both dead and dying. "So now" he waits in the hall, unable to escape the thought of watching the doctor "sew up." Though his son's death registers with little emotion—"So he's dead" (327)—the loss of the boy and Catherine becomes entangled with his own wounds, sewn together into Frederic's present articulation of their absences.

So active, so *now*, these deaths remain alive for Frederic. They hemorrhage through the narrative—reminders that while many are strong at the broken places, vulnerabilities remain. If, as Caruth observes, trauma emerges as "a kind of double telling, the oscillation between . . . the story of the unbearable nature of an event and the story of the unbearable nature of its survival" (*Unclaimed* 7), *A Farewell to Arms* constitutes just this kind of double telling. Driven by the tension between the "patient" and his prosthesis, between the "Me" who cries out on the operating table and the "I" who looks down and sees two broken bodies, Frederic's prosthetic narrative cannot mend his shattered past. In his unbearable present, any former understanding of the self seems hopelessly lost. As he himself notes about his Saint Anthony talisman, "After I was wounded I never found him" (44).

On his way to the battle that will see him wounded, Frederic considers the gift from Catherine: "The Saint Anthony was in a little white metal capsule. I opened the capsule and spilled him out into my hand" (43). He reassembles it, undoes his uniform, and puts the chain around his neck: "I felt him in his metal box against my chest while we drove. Then I forgot about him" (44). Spilled out and put back again, Saint Anthony goes to pieces but returns to wholeness in Frederic's hands, and in his retelling is again spilled out and put back, remembered though still missing. Like Frederic's narrative itself, Saint Anthony is both scar and open wound. And so *A Farewell to Arms*—an "aftereffect," a note marked "Urgent"—manifests a search for what is lost that cannot end.

Notes

1. I use the terms trauma and shell shock interchangeably, despite the fact that contemporary critics rightly insist on their historical situatedness along a convoluted path marked by stretches of collective forgetting and frenzied attention: from nineteenth-century theories about hysteria and railway spine to First World

War conceptions of shell shock, Second World War experiences with combat fatigue, the post-traumatic stress disorder (PTSD) of returning Vietnam veterans and survivors of incest and abuse, and, finally, present-day conceptions of the disorder that increasingly incorporate both neurophysiological and psychological models in research and treatment. Current understandings of trauma have come a long way from Great War–era debates over brain lesions and explosions as the roots of shell shock, but many congruencies remain between our understanding now and then, including a shared emphasis on disruptions to the embodied subject's relation to language, memory, and time. Much as it was during the Great War years, trauma theory today remains a deeply and bitterly contested field marked by controversy and competing theory. Moreover, shell shock and trauma both point out one thing that current research confirms and Frederic's narrative illustrates: any attempts to articulate shell shock, to put trauma into words, involves the unavoidable, unpredictable, and perhaps unknowable impress of the past on an embodied subject's present. For detailed treatments of the histories I have alluded to here, see Allan Young and Ruth Leys. Judith Herman's important and thorough *Trauma and Recovery* provides a feminist accounting of the history of trauma as well as an analysis of modes of treatment in the face of trauma's staying power. Ben Shephard offers a full-length, detailed history focused largely on military psychiatry that criticizes the current direction of trauma studies. Hans Binneveld offers a more concise and less polemical overview.

2. Armstrong explores the human body not only as a "locus of anxiety, even crisis" (4) but also as a site for recovery and regeneration through mechanical and technological intervention. Kirby Farrell extends Armstrong's terms outward from the human body, noting that prosthetic linkages between humans and society develop rapidly in the modernist period. For Farrell, trauma "reflects a disruption of our prosthetic relationships to the world. By exposing the constructed and interdependent nature of our existence, it makes vivid how radically vulnerable and ephemeral we are" (176). *A Farewell to Arms* stages shell shock's radical disrupting of subjectivity throughout a narrative that precisely testifies to the vulnerabilities of a self cut off from the web of prosthetic relations offering security and helping to locate meaning.

3. Hemingway's relations to the Great War and his own wounding are concerns that he returns to again and again in his career. Numerous critical attempts have been made to establish connections between the wartime experiences of the author and his Great War novel, suggesting links between memories that both author and protagonist seem unable to move beyond. For recent detailed treatments of Hemingway's construction of the novel, see Rena Sanderson, Charles Oliver, and Linda Wagner-Martin. Other important treatments of the novel include Michael Reynolds's *Hemingway's First War* and Bernard Stanley Oldsey. Matthew Stewart considers these matters in the wider context of Hemingway's entire career.

4. The early to mid-1990s witnessed an explosion of interdisciplinary interest in trauma. Critics such as Judith Herman, Shoshana Felman and Dori Laub, Cathy Caruth, Kali Tal, and Bessel A. van der Kolk and Onno van der Hart contributed

works that address the intersections of history, memory, medicine, psychoanalysis, and literature. Numerous anthologies also appeared, each marked by a particular approach or set of approaches: the psychoanalytically inflected *Trauma: Explorations in Memory* edited by Cathy Caruth, the juridical and scientific studies of *Trauma and Memory* edited by Paul Applebaum et al., the neurobiologically focused *Traumatic Stress* edited by van der Kolk et al., and the discursive identity politics of *Tense Past* edited by Paul Antze and Michael Lambek. Several recent anthologies productively merge trauma studies with other important domains such as comparative genocide studies, geopolitics, and the ethics of witnessing. See in particular *Extremities*, edited by Nancy K. Miller and Jason Tougaw; *Topologies of Trauma*, edited by Linda Belau and Peter Ramadanovic; *Trauma at Home*, edited by Judith Greenberg; and *Witness and Memory*, edited by Ana Douglass and Thomas A. Vogler.

While the works of Caruth and van der Kolk help in particular to focus my argument about *A Farewell to Arms*, it is important to acknowledge that their versions of traumatic operations have detractors. LaCapra, for instance, suggests that in the "affectively charged" (109) writing of Caruth, "trauma may itself be sacralized as a catastrophic revelation or, in more secular terms, be transvalued as the radical other or the sublime" (108). Such transvaluing can foreclose possibilities for working through by reifying trauma as fully and radically unknowable. And van der Kolk, in LaCapra's view, privileges neuroscience over the nuances of psychoanalysis: he relies on "an overly functional specific model of the brain" (109) and conveniently splits off "repression from dissociation and resists any notion of their connection" (108). Chapter-length critiques of Caruth and van der Kolk also appear in Leys, who charges both theorists with manipulative readings and research and disputes their claims about the literal truths of inscribed traumatic memories. However, the recent book by Jenny Edkins offers a direct challenge to Leys's critique of Caruth, charging Leys herself with manipulative misreading:

> It is not the case that "truth" is said to exist in the memory images thought to be implanted by trauma any more than it is to be found in our original perceptions. We do not have access to these images (other than as images) without interpreting or making sense of them. We cannot pass them on unvarnished to others. (39)

As for van der Kolk, Leys's charges notwithstanding, there is much to be found in the work of other trauma theorists—Babette Rothschild, Bruce D. Perry, and Belleruth Naparstek, for example—to support the notion that traumatic experience invokes both mind and body. Perry writes:

> All areas of the brain and body are recruited and orchestrated for optimal survival tasks during the threat. This total neurobiological participation in the threat response is important in understanding how a traumatic experience can impact and alter functioning in such a pervasive fashion. Cognitive, emotional, social, behavioral and physiological residues of a trauma may impact an individual for years—even a lifetime. (14)

As it happens, my own critique of Caruth's work may be leveled here. After Freud, who suggests in *Beyond the Pleasure Principle* that wounds or injuries suffered in the context of a frightful surprise tend to work "against the development of a neurosis" (12), Caruth contends that "the wound of the mind—the breach in the mind's experience of time, self, and the world—is not, like the wound of the body, a simple and healable event" (*Unclaimed Experience* 4). Her privileging of mind over body, of psychic wounds over physical ones, however, leaves largely out of the picture the upshot of some of the most interesting conclusions about the impact of trauma on the embodied subject. In contrast, Frederic's narrative presciently considers the interpenetration of mind and body in the wake of traumatic experiences and problematizes the notion of wounds of any sort as "simple and healable event[s]."

5. Fine work by Mary Prescott and James Nagel, for instance, gestures toward trauma in the context of Frederic's narrative efforts. Prescott explores the processes by which Frederic reconstructs events "so that he can make sense of them" (43). Along similar lines, Nagel considers Frederic's retrospective efforts at "coming to terms emotionally with the events" (171). But neither essay follows through on the narrative aftereffects in Frederic's version of his past.

6. Margot Norris suggests that *A Farewell to Arms* is "less a novel about war than a novel as war" (693) and provides a particularly illuminating connection to what trauma theorists document as the aggressive operations of trauma. She convincingly argues that Hemingway's text delivers acts of "narrative aggression" (694) that refigure, in rhetorical terms, "the aggression of combat" (695). Norris reads inconsistencies and ruptures in the novel as coercive efforts to efface responsibility for the violence of war, and I read them as evidence of the suffering of profound traumas. To paraphrase Norris herself, *A Farewell to Arms* is less a novel about trauma than a novel as trauma.

The works of Lisa Tyler and Richard Badenhausen might also be considered here in the context of Frederic's trauma narrative. In Tyler's article Frederic masters his trauma by "making of it an ordered narrative" (91). While I do agree that Frederic's retelling of his losses should be considered in terms of efforts at resistance and as a measure of healing, to suggest that his narrative "triumphs over trauma" (91) is to overlook the extent to which his past relentlessly continues to intrude on his present in ways that I contend are beyond his control. Badenhausen analyzes Vera Brittain's *Testament of Youth* as a "working through" of the trauma of her wartime losses. Though the redemptive nature of this reading does not help me to account for what I perceive in *A Farewell to Arms* as the continued debilitating effects of trauma that work at denying the satisfactions of closure, Badenhausen's work nonetheless provides compelling analysis of the workings of trauma with respect to narrative.

7. Phelan insists that with "few exceptions, Frederic speaks from his perspective at the time of the action" (68). Reynolds suggests that "the only difference between Frederic in the nurse's garden and in the Milan hospital is his violent wounding. Like a victim of shell shock, he exhibits altered feelings, affection, temper, and habits" ("Doctors" 120). Like Phelan, Reynolds assumes that the novel operates

in terms of a pre- and post-wounding dynamic, but I suggest that there is no way to untangle Frederic's post-traumatic narration from his present version of the past.

8. Another key source for interpreting his injury remains the *Diagnostic and Statistical Manual of Mental Disorders*. In the manual's terms, PTSD may develop in those who have been exposed to extreme events or stressors "involving direct personal experience of an event that involves actual or threatened death or serious injury, or other threat to one's physical integrity; or witnessing an event that involves death, injury, or a threat to the physical integrity of another person; or learning about unexpected or violent death, serious harm, or threat of death or injury experienced by a family member or other close associate." (463)

Frederic, an ambulance driver on the Austro-Italian front, remains consistently exposed, both directly and indirectly, to such events. Even a partial list will suggest the extremes involved. Blown up and wounded himself, he attends to Passini: "One leg was gone and the other was held by tendons and part of the trouser and the stump twitched and jerked as though it were not connected" (55). Participating in the massive Italian retreat from Caporetto, Frederic loses one of his men, beloved Aymo: "He was hit low in the back of the neck and the bullet had ranged upward and come out under the right eye. He died while I was stopping up the two holes" (213). Threatened with summary execution for his officer's rank, Frederic evades rifle fire by plunging into the river: "I thought then I would drown because of my boots, but I thrashed and fought through the water, and when I looked up the bank was coming toward me, and I kept thrashing and swimming in a heavy-footed panic until I reached it." (227)

And finally, Frederic loses his son—"cord was caught around his neck or something" (327)—only hours before he loses his partner: "It seems she had one hemorrhage after another. They couldn't stop it. I went into the room and stayed with Catherine until she died. She was unconscious all the time, and it did not take her very long to die" (331).

9. Babette Rothschild's work in *The Body Remembers: Casebook* suggests that during a traumatic incident the brain's limbic system signals to the sympathetic nervous system (SNS) for preparation to fight or fly; if neither of these options seems appropriate, the parasympathetic nervous system (PNS) initiates the freeze response: "The SNS continues its extreme arousal while the PNS freezes the action of the body" (6). Although freezing "only occurs when the individual's perception is that the threat is extreme and escape impossible" (7), Rothschild speculates that the toll on the "frozen" subject—including intense feelings of shame and humiliation—may be greater afterward because of the lingering belief that more could have been done.

10. Rothschild notes that PTSD's long-term aftereffects may damage or destroy a survivor's ability to differentiate between external stimuli and to make use of the body's signals to itself regarding threats: The ability to orient to safety and danger becomes decreased when many things, or sometimes everything, in the environment are perceived as dangerous. When daily reminders of trauma become extreme, freezing or dissociation can be activated as if the trauma were occurring in the present. It can become a vicious cycle. (*Psychophysiology* 14)

11. Concerned mostly with the (in)visibility of the disabled body, Davis offers a stirring condemnation of the "reception of disability" that structures the art world's perceptions and attitudes about "the presence of difference" (56) and the "traditional ableist assumptions" (52) that permeate virtually all corridors of Western life. He suggests that any conception of the body as a whole is based on "a repression of the fragmentary nature of the body" (59) as it is experienced early in one's psychic and physiological development and reinforced by a culture deeply invested in this repression.

12. I am extremely grateful for Laura Tanner's guidance and efforts at every stage in the writing of this essay. The insights offered by Rosemarie Bodenheimer and James Krasner along the way are also much appreciated. As ever, I extend my deepest thanks to Amy Winchester for her constant support and encouragement.

Works cited

Antze, Paul, and Michael Lambek, eds. *Tense Past: Cultural Essays in Trauma and Memory*. New York: Routledge, 1996.

Appelbaum, Paul S., Lisa A. Uyehara, and Mark R. Elin, eds. *Trauma and Memory: Clinical and Legal Controversies*. New York: Oxord UP, 1997.

Armstrong, Tim. *Modernism, Technology, and the Body: A Cultural Study*. Cambridge: Cambridge UP, 1998.

Badenhausen, Richard. "Mourning Through Memoir: Trauma, Testimony, and Community in Vera Brittain's Testament of Youth." *Twentieth-Century Literature* 49.4 (Winter 2003): 421–48.

Belau, Linda, and Petar Ramadanovic, eds. *Topologies of Trauma: Essays on the Limit of Knowledge and Memory*. New York: Other, 2002.

Binneveld, Hans. *From Shell Shock to Combat Stress: A Comparative History of Military Psychology*. Trans. John O'Kane. Amsterdam: Amsterdam UP, 1997.

Bourke, Joanna. *An Intimate History of Killing: Face-to-Face Killing in Twentieth-Century Warfare*. New York: Basic, 1999.

Caruth, Cathy, ed. *Trauma: Explorations in Memory.* Baltimore: Johns Hopkins UP, 1995.

————. *Unclaimed Experience: Trauma, Narrative, and History.* Baltimore: Johns Hopkins UP, 1996.

Davis, Lennard J. "Nude Venuses, Medusa's Body, and Phantom Limbs: Disability and Visuality." *The Body and Physical Difference: Discourses of Disability.* Ed. David T. Mitchell and Sharon L. Snyder. Ann Arbor: U of Michigan P, 1997. 51–70.

Diagnostic and Statistical Manual of Mental Disorders. 4th ed. Washington, D.C.: American Psychiatric Association, 2000.

Douglass, Ana, and Thomas A. Vogler, eds. *Witness and Memory: The Discourse of Trauma.* New York: Routledge, 2003.

Edkins, Jenny. *Trauma and the Memory of Politics.* Cambridge: Cambridge UP, 2003.

Farrell, Kirby. *Post-Traumatic Culture: Injury and Interpretation in the Nineties.* Baltimore: Johns Hopkins UP, 1998.

Felman, Shoshana, and Dori Laub. *Testimony: Crises of Witnessing in Literature, Psychoanalysis, and History.* New York: Routledge, 1992.

Freud, Sigmund. *Beyond the Pleasure Principle.* 1920. Trans. James Strachey. *The Standard Edition of the Complete Psychological Works of Sigmund Freud.* vol. 18. London: Hogarth, 1955. 7–66.

Fussell, Paul. *The Great War and Modern Memory.* London: Oxford UP, 1975.

Greenberg, Judith, ed. *Trauma at Home: After 9/11.* Lincoln: U of Nebraska P, 2003.

Grosz, Elizabeth. *Volatile Bodies: Toward a Corporeal Feminism.* Bloomington: Indiana UP, 1994.

Hemingway, Ernest. *A Farewell to Arms.* New York: Scribner's, 1995.

Herman, Judith Lewis. *Trauma and Recovery.* New York: Basic, 1992.

Herndl, Diane Price. "Invalid Masculinity: Silence, Hospitals, and Anaesthesia in *A Farewell to Arms.*" *Hemingway Review* 21.1 (Fall 2001): 38–52.

Injuries and Diseases of War: A Manual Based on Experience of the Present Campaign in France. London: His Majesty's Stationery Office, 1918.

LaCapra, Dominick. *Writing History, Writing Trauma.* Baltimore: Johns Hopkins UP, 2001.

Leys, Ruth. *Trauma: A Genealogy.* Chicago: U of Chicago P, 2000.

Miller, Nancy K., and Jason Tougaw, eds. *Extremities: Trauma, Testimony, and Community.* Urbana: U of Chicago P, 2002.

Nagel, James. "Catherine Barkley and Retrospective Narration in *A Farewell to Arms.*" *Ernest Hemingway: Six Decades of Criticism.* Ed. Linda W. Wagner. East Lansing: Michigan State UP, 1987. 171–85.

Naparstek, Belleruth. *Invisible Heroes: Survivors of Trauma and How They Heal.* New York: Bantam, 2004.

Norris, Margot. "The Novel as War: Lies and Truth in Hemingway's *A Farewell to Arms.*" *Modern Fiction Studies* 40.4 (1994): 689–710.

Oldsey, Bernard Stanley. *Hemingway's Hidden Craft: The Writing of* A Farewell to Arms. University Park: Pennsylvania State UP, 1979.

Oliver, Charles, ed. *Ernest Hemingway's* A Farewell to Arms: *A Documentary Volume.* Detroit: Thomson, 2005.

Perry, Bruce D. "The Memories of States: How the Brain Stores and Retrieves Traumatic Experience." *Splintered Reflections: Images of the Body in Trauma.* Ed. Jean Goodwin and Reina Attias. New York: Basic, 1999. 9–38.

Phelan, James. "Distance, Voice, and Temporal Perspective in Frederic Henry's Narration: Successes, Problems, and Paradox." *New Essays on* A Farewell to Arms. Ed. Scott Donaldson. Cambridge: Cambridge UP, 1990. 53–73.

Prescott, Mary. "*A Farewell to Arms*: Memory and the Perpetual Now." *College Literature* 17.1 (1990): 41–52.

Reynolds, Michael. "*A Farewell to Arms*: Doctors in the House of Love." *The Cambridge Companion to Hemingway.* Ed. Scott Donaldson. Cambridge: Cambridge UP, 1996. 109–27. New York: Blackwell, 1987.

Rothschild, Babette. *The Body Remembers: Casebook.* New York: Norton, 2003.

———. *The Body Remembers: The Psychophysiology of Trauma and Trauma Treatment.* New York: Norton, 2000.

Sanderson, Rena, ed. *Hemingway's Italy: New Perspectives.* Baton Rouge: Louisiana State UP, 2006.

Scarry, Elaine. *The Body in Pain: The Making and Unmaking of the World.* New York: Oxford UP, 1985.

Shephard, Ben. *A War of Nerves: Soldiers and Psychiatrists in the Twentieth Century.* Cambridge: Harvard UP, 2000.

Stewart, Matthew C. "Ernest Hemingway and World War I: Combatting Recent Psychobiographical Reassessments, Restoring the War." *Papers on Language and Literature: A Journal for Scholars and Critics of Language and Literature* 36.2 (Spring 2000): 198–217.

Tal, Kali. *Worlds of Hurt: Reading the Literatures of Trauma.* Cambridge: Cambridge UP, 1996.

Tate, Trudi. *Modernism, History, and the First World War.* Manchester: Manchester UP, 1998.

Tyler, Lisa. "Passion and Grief in *A Farewell to Arms*: Ernest Hemingway's Retelling of Wuthering Heights." *Hemingway Review* 14.2 (Spring 1995): 79–96.

van der Kolk, Bessel A., Alexander C. McFarlane, and Lars Weisaeth, eds. *Traumatic Stress: The Effects of Overwhelming Experience on Mind, Body, and Society.* New York: Guilford, 1996.

van der Kolk, Bessel A., and Onno van der Hart. "The Intrusive Past: The Flexibility of Memory and the Engraving of Trauma." *Trauma: Explorations in Memory.* Ed. Cathy Caruth. Baltimore: Johns Hopkins UP, 1995. 158–82.

Wagner-Martin, Linda. Ernest Hemingway's *A Farewell to Arms: A Reference Guide.* Westport: Greenwood, 2003.

Wills, David. *Prosthesis.* Stanford: Stanford UP, 1995.

Young, Allan. *The Harmony of Illusions: Inventing Post-Traumatic Stress Disorder.* Princeton: Princeton UP, 1995.

Young, James E. "Between History and Memory: The Voice of the Eyewitness." *Witness and Memory: The Discourse of Trauma.* Ed. Ana Douglass and Thomas A. Vogler. New York: Routledge, 2003. 275–83.

The Religion of Death in
A Farewell to Arms

James F. Light

James F. Light was an English professor.

In the following viewpoint, Light explains that in the novel
A Farewell to Arms, *Frederic Henry encounters four characters
who each present a different ideal of service—religious service
from the priest, patriotism from Gino, selfless love from Catherine, and service to mankind from Rinaldi. Light maintains that
over the course of the novel, Frederic examines each type of service for its benefits as an ideal to live by, but in the end rejects
each of them as inadequate means of dominating death, the one
thing that all men attempt to conquer in their lifetime. In the
end, Light believes that* A Farewell to Arms *concludes that humans can only gain a sense of immortality by maintaining their
bravery and stoicism when confronted with death, thus making
these convictions the only form of religion worth believing.*

One way of looking at Ernest Hemingway's *A Farewell to
Arms* is to see its close involvement in four ideals of service.[1] Each of these ideals is dramatized by a character of
some importance, and it is between these four that Lt. Henry
wavers in the course of the novel. The orthodoxly religious
ideal of service is that of the priest, who wishes to serve God
but who asserts as well the broader concept of service: "When
you love you wish to do things for. You wish to sacrifice for.
You wish to serve."[2] Another selfless ideal of service is that of
the patriot Gino, who wishes to serve his country so fully that
he is willing to die for it. A third is the code of Catherine Ber-

James F. Light, "The Religion of Death in *A Farewell to Arms*," *Modern Fiction Studies*,
vol. 7, Summer 1961, pp. 169–173. Copyright © 1961 by Modern Fiction Studies. All
rights reserved. Reproduced by permission.

keley [*sic*], who wishes to serve her lover and who sees in such service her personal substitute for conventional religion. The last is the ideal of Rinaldi, who, as a doctor, wishes to serve mankind by alleviating the wounds of war. Each is an initiate to the subordination of self, and in this they differ from the selfishness of the king and the officers who ride in cars and throw mud on the men, or from the hero Ettore, who sees war as an accident suitable for promotion and self-glorification. In no other way, despite the contention of such a perceptive and influential critic as Robert Penn Warren, are they really initiates. They are not so in their greater discipline—Catherine is hysterical early in the novel and Rinaldi is a nervous wreck in the middle. They are not so in their talk, for though Rinaldi and Valentini, another doctor and another so-called initiate, may possess a similar "bantering, ironical tone," the priest and Catherine are far removed from any such tone; nor do they have any greater awareness than others "of the issue of meaning in life."[3] They act instinctively rather than intellectually, and the one instinct they have in common—the attraction toward the ideal of service—is, from the context and the conclusion of the novel, a foolish selflessness without intellectual worth.

The priest, Gino, Catherine, and Rinaldi do, however, live by the ideal of service, and the dramatic tension of the novel is largely based on Lt. Henry's wavering toward each ideal and eventual rejection of all four. Toward the priest's ideal, Henry's attitude is at first not one of sympathy but of rejection. He does not bait the priest with the other priest-baiters early in the novel, but neither does he stay with the priest when the other officers leave for the whore houses nearby. Nor does he visit the high, cold, dry country, the priest's home, where he is invited to go on his leave. Instead he goes to the large cities, the ironic "centres of culture and civilization" (p. 8), where he lives the life of sensation and feels "that this was all and all and all and not caring" (p. 13). After he is wounded and has

Gary Cooper, as Frederic Henry, and Helen Hayes, as Catherine Barkley, in a touching scene from the 1932 film version of Hemingway's A Farewell to Arms. © Bettmann/Corbis.

found real love with Catherine, however, Lt. Henry comes closer to the priest, so that when he returns to duty he can reject the priest-baiting of Rinaldi and instead of going to town—and the whore houses—he can visit with the priest. The implication apparently is that the love Henry has found in Catherine has somehow made him more sympathetic to the kind of selfless love that the priest avows. By the end of the novel, however, Henry has thoroughly rejected the priest and his ideal of service to God. He does, however, give that ideal a test. Where the priest had earlier prayed for the end of the war—"I believe and I pray that something will happen. I have felt it very close" (pp. 184–5)—Henry now prays that Catherine not die. Basic and repetitive in the prayer is the implication of some necessary reciprocal relation between man and God: You do this for me and I'll do this for you. Thus Henry prays: "Oh, God, please don't let her die. I'll do anything for you if you won't let her die. . . . Please, please, please don't let her die. . . . I'll do anything you say if you don't make her die" (p. 341). Catherine, however, does die, just as, despite the priest's prayers, the war continues. The implication is that the priest's ideal of service lacks reciprocity, and the knowledge of its lack is not unique to Henry. Huck Finn had earlier, in the novel that Hemingway has said is the origin of all modern American literature, felt the same flaw; for he had seen, by pragmatic test, the inefficacy of prayer, and he had discerned that the priest's—or Miss Watson's—ideal of service was a one-way street with no advantage for the human individual. For Lt. Henry this lack of reciprocity makes for the image of a god who in his eternal selfishness is the origin of human selfishness, so that man in his selfishness most accurately reflects God. This concept of the divine selfishness is portrayed in Henry's remembrance, as Catherine is dying, of watching some ants burning on a log. Henry envisions the opportunity for him to be "a messiah and lift the log off the fire" (p. 339). Divinity, however, does not ease the pain of man's existence, and Henry does not save the ants. Instead, selfishly—and in so doing he is reflecting the divine selfishness which is so antithetical to the priest's ideal of service—Henry throws "a tin cup of water on the log, so that I would have the cup empty to put whiskey in before I added water to it" (p. 339).

A second ideal of service is that dramatized by the patriot Gino. He believes the "soil is sacred" (p. 190) and that the deaths in the war were not "in vain" (p. 191). He will not talk of losing the war and Lt. Henry feels he understands Gino's "being a patriot. He was born one" (p. 191). Though Lt. Henry never has Gino's simple love of country, he does for a good part of the novel act and talk as a "patriot." The priest applies the term to Lt. Henry (p. 74), and its justification, despite the fact that Lt. Henry is not more important both are involved in the service of healing man's body. After Henry has been wounded and has returned to duty, however, there is a change.

Henry finds that the priest now is more sure of himself, while Rinaldi, convinced that he has syphilis, is tense and irritable. The cause for the change is the way in which the war has been going. Many men have been killed and many wounded, and these facts have made the priest—concerned with man's soul— feel more necessary, while at the same time, they have made Rinaldi—concerned with man's body—feel his own futility. The difference is made clear when Rinaldi attempts to bait the priest, as in earlier days, and is unsuccessful in weakening the priest's placidity. His lack of success, though his insults go even beyond those of the earlier time, and his feeling that Henry is betraying him and is now on the priest's side enrage Rinaldi, and he yells at Henry that he can't side with the priest: "You can't do it. You can't do it. I say you can't do it. You're dry and you're empty and there's nothing else. There's nothing else I tell you. Not a damned thing. I know, when I stop working" (p. 180). The complete materialist—he calls himself "the snake of reason" (p. 176)—Rinaldi, after this scene, disappears physically from the novel, but his role as the worker for the cure of man's body is assumed later by another doctor, the one who cares for Catherine in her childbirth. Like Rinaldi, this doctor is also ineffectual in his attempt at service, and his feeling of his failure leads to apologetics which Henry rejects. Henry is left with the failure of all the ideals of service. In addition he is left with the knowledge of the one thing man can believe in: death. Catherine becomes a "statue"—which suggests some pagan deity—and the novel ends on the word *rain*, a word which symbolically stands for two things, paradoxically intertwined, in the novel. One is spring and new birth. The other is the thaws of spring that begin the war anew and anew bring death. In the beginning of life, then, is the fact of death, and the sexual urge is the bio-logical trap which leads to death. Death is the basic fact of life, and there is nothing more deserving of worship.

It is no wonder that in Hemingway's next book, *Death in the Afternoon*, he states—and it is a thorough rejection of any ideal of service—that "what is moral is what you feel good after and what is immoral is what you feel bad after."[4] Hemingway feels good after seeing a bullfight, and for him it is "very moral."[5] The reason is that in the bullfight one confronts in a pure way the ultimate fact of death. Man's problem is to dominate death as the bullfighter's is to dominate the bull, and the way toward domination is to see life, like the bullfight, as an art form, with certain rules which the "manly" man will obey. The basic offense against the "rules" of the bullfight is for the bullfighter to pretend to be in the area of danger while in reality he avoids that area and is perfectly safe. The basic offense against the "rules" of life as an art form is to show self-pity, an offense so great that Hemingway could, when he saw it in his friend F. Scott Fitzgerald, write a reprimanding letter in which he pointed out that all men "are bitched from the start" and no man has any right to whine.[6] To avoid the area of danger in the bullfight is to avoid real domination of the bull; to whine in life is to avoid domination of death. The lack of domination makes for messiness—impure art—in either the bullfight or life. Such messiness is a form of cheating, and in life "when you get the damned hurt use it—don't cheat with it."[7]

Watching the bullfights, Hemingway gains a feeling of "life and death, mortality and immortality."[8] Though he himself is vague about the reason he gains these feelings, it seems clear that the feeling of immortality does not come from any orthodox Christian reason. Instead it arises because the bullfighter, when he enters the area of danger, shows his contempt for death, becomes victorious over it, and gains in his victory a small immortality. The same kind of contempt for death is evident in the way in which Catherine meets her end, for she recognizes her death as a "dirty trick" (p. 342) but winks at the joke. She has not been broken by death, despite her feeling to the contrary, and she has therefore gained victory and immortality. This is the only kind of immortality man can know; it is gained by bravery and stoicism, not selfless service to God (the priest), country (Gino), beloved (Catherine), or mankind (Rinaldi). Such a limited immortality is a poor substitute for victory over death through everlasting life; but it is the only kind of immortality, the only kind of religion, the Hemingway of *Farewell* can believe in.

1. Robert Penn Warren discusses two of these ideals, those of Catherine and the priest, in his introduction to Scribner's "Modern Standard Authors" edition of *Farewell*. Anyone familiar with Mr. Warren's essay will see that though I disagree with much of its interpretation of *Farewell*, I at the same time am indebted to it deeply.

2. Ernest Hemingway, *A Farewell to Arms*, Intro. Robert Penn Warren (Scribner's "Modern Standard Authors," 1949), p. 75. Subsequent page references to *Farewell* are from this edition and are incorporated in the text.

3. Warren, Introduction to Hemingway's *A Farewell to Arms*, p. xxxi.

4. Ernest Hemingway, *Death in the Afternoon*, (Scribner's, 1932), p. 4.

5. Hemingway, *Death in the Afternoon*, p. 4.

6. Letter from Ernest Hemingway to F. Scott Fitzgerald. Quoted in Arthur Mizener, *The Far Side of Paradise* (Houghton-Mifflin, 1951), p. 238.

7. Letter from Hemingway to Fitzgerald. Quoted in Mizener, *The Far Side of Paradise*, p. 238.

8. Hemingway, *Death in the Afternoon*, p. 4.

Social Issues in Literature

CHAPTER 3

Contemporary Perspectives on War

Dying for Humanity Has Replaced Dying for God, King, or Country in Modern War

Michael Howard

Michael Howard was a history professor at both Oxford and Yale Universities and is life president of the International Institute for Strategic Studies.

In the following viewpoint, Howard traces the evolution of warfare justification and argues that today, instead of fighting for one's god, king, or country, modern militaries and soldiers instead must fight for a transnational system in which the war is fought for humanity's benefit. In tracing this evolution, Howard examines the motivation needed to encourage soldiers to fight. He identifies four main motivating factors throughout time that have led militaries to war—in the name of god, king, country, and liberty. Each of these factors has given way to the next and created the modern situation in which the only justifiable reason for going to war, in the author's view, is to protect the security of the globalized world where all individuals' well-being and happiness depend upon transnational order. Howard admits that this global policing provides much less impetus for soldiers to fight and die than the historical motivations, but he insists that the justifications for war today must be relevant to modern times.

> *Pale Ebenezer thought it wrong to fight. But Battling Bill (who slew him) thought it right.*
>
> *—Hilaire Belloc*

Hilaire Belloc [an Anglo-French writer] penned this sardonic couplet in those halcyon days before 1914 when, in Europe and North America, "the Peace Movement" was reaching its height. The rest of the twentieth century, with its unprecedented bloodshed and catastrophic results, might seem to justify the views of Ebenezer. Is the world any better, we may ask, as a result of all those wars? Should people not have listened to him rather than to Battling Bill and, like him, refused to fight? Today Ebenezer's successors continue gallantly to urge their cause; and even if they have failed to persuade us that to fight is "wrong," at least we now expect our governments to think a great deal harder before they put their soldiers (as the rather-charming American euphemism has it) "in harm's way": that is, order them to kill people and run a distinct risk of getting killed themselves.

In considering the reasons that people give, and have given in the past, for killing one another, I have in mind something rather different from the justification, the *jus ad bellum* [right to war], that governments give when they go to war. Rather, it is the justification invoked by the people who do the actual killing; that exemption from the normal laws of humanity which licenses, indeed orders, them to do things that would otherwise be considered abominable. If we look for the answer in the history of the Western world, we find it conveniently summarized in the motto under which the British army went to war in 1914: for God, king and country. But nowadays the first of those authorities, if He is invoked at all, is likely to provoke contention rather than unity. The second has little significance even where such a person still exists. Finally, in a global and interdependent world order, even the demand "to die for one's country" has lost much of its appeal; more so perhaps in a Europe battered after two bruising world wars than in a victorious and still-intact United States.

Further, although it is conceivable that wars may still have to be fought for territorial defense, in practice those in which

135

the United States and her allies have engaged for the past half century have consisted of the projection of armed force to distant parts of the world to engage in conflicts that, although fought in "the national interest," often bear a very remote connection to the actual defense of one's native land. Sometimes the connecting thread seems very tenuous indeed. Under such circumstances a new and stronger argument may be needed to provide a convincing license to kill.

Fighting for God Breeds Professional Soldiers

The triad of "God, king and country" offers a useful summary of the reasons that people in the Western world have given for killing one another over the past thousand years. Like most historians, I assume a central "Westphalian" period in European history, dating from the Peace of Westphalia in 1648 [that ended both the Thirty Years' War and the Eighty Years' War] and lasting into the twentieth, if not the twenty-first, century, that began when Europe sorted itself out into the system of sovereign states which has been the template for international relations until our own time. Before that we find a "feudal" era, when relations between political powers were vertical rather than horizontal. Then, all political authority was seen as being ultimately derived from God, from whom it devolved through a pyramid of authorities, all of whom claimed by derivation to act as His agents; a claim ratified by the sanction of a universal church. When these authorities fought between themselves—as they did almost continuously—they did so to uphold, or restore, a divinely ordained order, and could thus invoke divine sanction to justify their claims. In practice, their conflicts were usually struggles over possession or inheritance of landed property. For them war was a form of litigation, an appeal to God's judgment, and fighting was the means of ensuring that His will should be done. The people who did the fighting usually did so to fulfill their obligations to an overlord who rewarded them with land and the political power that went with it; but in any case they were born to warfare, thoroughly enjoyed it and had little else to do with their time.

When they were not fighting among themselves, Christians engaged in a more existential conflict against what they saw as incarnate powers of evil, the Muslims; adversaries whose encroachments threatened the entire structure of Western Christendom for the best part of a thousand years, from the eighth well into the eighteenth century. It was a conflict that saw Muslim armies penetrate deep into France and Christian crusaders establish themselves in Palestine, and that persisted in southeast Europe well into the nineteenth century. For Christians the justification for killing, and if necessary dying, in combat with such an adversary seemed self-evident. Their adversaries fought with similar enthusiasm for their own conception of God. All too many of them still do.

For Western Europe, however, the menace of the Muslims eventually waned, leaving behind a large class of *désoeuvré* [idle] warriors who knew no other way of earning their living. These fighters formed themselves into mercenary bands and placed their swords at the disposal of anyone who would pay for them. For them war was no longer a means of serving God, but a straightforward trade. They were professionals. Their loyalty was to their own group leader. They served whoever employed them so long as they were paid. If they were not paid they did not fight. But so long as they were paid, they were content to kill or be killed. Their motivation was pure professional pride.

Kings' Authority Depends on Money, Not God

These professionals eventually found steady employment in serving the dynasties who achieved dominance over Europe in the later Middle Ages and were anointed by a complaisant church, on the Judaic model, as "kings": a status that was seen to place them in a direct relationship with God. The feudal pyramid gradually disappeared, and these monarchs assumed the sole right to "make war" and demand the obedience of their subjects in so doing; thus providing that all-important element in the Christian *jus ad bellum*: "right authority." This royal authority was still allegedly derived from a divine source—in serving one's king one was serving God—but the Westphalian era had now begun. The feudal hierarchy based on obedience to a pyramid of overlords evolved into a "system of states" in which monarchs were the sole judges of the legitimacy of their cause and from whom there was no appeal, either upward to God or downward to "the people." Kings required no justification for their wars beyond the need to protect or extend their own power, or occasionally to preserve "the balance of power"; an objective explicitly invoked to justify the upkeep of the British army until the middle of the nineteenth century.

But although they might claim their ultimate authority from God as "anointed kings," the power of these monarchs still depended on military force. This required that they should successfully convert the existing mercenary bands into disciplined and loyal armed forces; which they could do only if they found the money to pay them. It was largely to ensure a regular source of income to do this that European monarchs created the mechanism of taxation and representation that became known as "the state." The English political thinker Thomas Hobbes was to call the state a "Leviathan" describing it as "that Mortall God," "our peace and defense"—a secular authority that replaced the rather less effective Immortal God in providing security for its members. With the resources of such states at their disposal, monarchs were now able, from the mid-seventeenth century until the end of the eighteenth, to wage wars much as they willed, with professional armed forces who killed one another and got themselves killed in the

US Army recruiting poster shows a soldier standing next to an American flag and blowing a bugle. Fighting to defend one's country was once used as motivation for going to war, but in modern times fighting to defend humanity has replaced fighting for love of country. © GL Archive / Alamy.

name of the king to whom they swore allegiance and who paid them; not caring very much whether or not he derived his authority from God.

Dying for Country Usurps Dying for God or King

Then peoples began to discover that, so long as the mechanism of the state functioned effectively, kings themselves were expendable. A new concept of loyalty gradually took shape; one to a community with which people could more directly identify themselves. In this development the British led the way. There an unpopular King James II was expelled in 1689, and little reverence was felt for his foreign successors. The British army formally swore allegiance to the monarch, but in practice developed that fanatical loyalty to specific regiments which survives to this day, while the sailors who won command of the seas in the great wars against France fought not so much for their king as for their "country"; a concept that would be inherited by their cousins in North America a few years later when they discarded the royal connection altogether.

The territorial concept of "country" is interestingly distinct both from the term "nation" in whose name the French were to dispose of their own king, and even more from that which was to so profoundly stir their German neighbors, "*volk*": a quasi-metaphysical concept associated with *blut* rather than *boden*, blood rather than soil, and one of which the English word "people" can give only a misleading and inadequate impression. To these terms were to be added the classical and familial *patrie, patria* and "fatherland." These differences in terminology provide an interesting insight into the cultural distinctions that were beginning to reveal themselves as the peoples of Europe gradually developed self-awareness; to analyze them adequately would demand a very large book; but what they all shared was universality and immense emotional force.

The universality was important in an increasingly secular age when a dwindling number of people were prepared to die simply for God, and an even more rapidly dwindling minority were prepared to lay down their lives for their king, even assuming that they still had one. Armies now consisted increasingly of volunteers or conscripts who needed a motivation that would inspire them all, regardless of class or creed. As the traditional foci of loyalty faded, they were replaced by the far more powerful concepts that were to fuel the great national wars of the nineteenth and twentieth centuries, in which young men were to die and kill for their "country" or "fatherland"; though when possible, as we have seen, "God" and "king" were bracketed with it in an all-embracing trinity.

Enlightenment Wars Are Still Fought for Country

But by the twentieth century we are entering a third, or post-Westphalian era: that of what might be termed "Enlightenment Wars." The savants of the eighteenth-century Enlightenment had argued that war, so far from being an inevitable if not positively desirable element in human affairs, was an unnecessary evil created by the self-interest of monarchs and their attendant aristocrats who then ruled the peoples of Europe. Wars were thus justifiable, they argued, only if they were fought to liberate peoples from these oppressive regimes, whether they were homegrown or foreign imposed. The first such war for what would now be termed "regime change" was that commenced by the French revolutionary government in response to the allied invasion of 1793, when the French invaded their neighbors to liberate them from monarchical oppression; a rationale that inspired the armies of Napoleon Bonaparte to carry the flag of liberty, equality and fraternity throughout a rather ungrateful Europe. This set the pattern for "wars of liberation" fought during the nineteenth century to free the Greeks, the Italians and the peoples of the Balkan peninsula from oppressive Austrian or Ottoman rule. It was a concept that received its full epiphany in 1917, when President Woodrow Wilson took the United States into the First World

War, proclaiming that America would fight not, like the European powers, simply for her own national interest but "for democracy, for the right of those who submit to authority to have a voice in their own governments, for the rights and liberties of small nations, for a universal dominion of right by such a concert of free peoples as shall bring peace and safety to all nations and make the world itself free." The conflict between Pale Ebenezer and Battling Bill now seemed resolved: The justification for going to war was to bring war itself to an end.

But although the democracies triumphed in 1918, their peoples still proved very reluctant to fight enlightenment wars. The Americans dissociated themselves from Wilson's "concert of free peoples," the League of Nations, with all the uncomfortable obligations that membership would have involved. The French and British refused even to contemplate war against Japan in 1931 or Italy in 1935 when those states invaded and subjugated peaceful peoples in defiance of their international obligations. When France and Britain did eventually go to war in 1939, their immediate justifications were in principle purely "Westphalian": to fulfill treaty obligations and maintain a balance of power; but fundamentally their peoples agreed to fight because they realized that their "countries" were now in danger. The United States and the Soviet Union remained aloof even longer, and entered the war only when they were themselves physically attacked. Whatever the rhetoric of their leaders, the vast majority of the people who actually fought those wars did not do so for democracy or fascism or communism. They simply fought, as they had a generation earlier, for their "countries"; the Americans as much as everyone else.

Nevertheless, whether or not the American people believed that they had been fighting an enlightenment war for a better world, at the end of it President [Franklin D.] Roosevelt was better placed than had been any of his predecessors to insist upon a truly enlightenment peace; that is, the establishment of a community of self-governing democracies, by definition peace-loving, who would go to war only to restore the international order if it were threatened by a "rogue state." Five years later, when North Korea invaded its southern neighbor, the United Nations actually did so. National armies then fought, however notionally, under a United Nations flag. But it was still assumed that such wars would be fought between *states*. Their object was to preserve an international order in which the only serious actors would be states who still enjoyed, as [German sociologist and philosopher] Max Weber had put it, a "monopoly on violence." To that extent the system was still "Westphalian": Peace would be kept and order maintained by interstate agreements. Those who fought these enlightenment wars, if called upon to do so, would do so because their state so ordered, albeit in a higher cause. So far as the armed forces themselves were concerned, they were still fighting for their country.

Wars for Transnational Order Have Taken Over

Then came the appalling atrocity of 9/11 [referring to the September 11, 2001, terrorist attacks on the United States]. This foreshadowed an entirely new era; one in which states could be threatened, and international order disrupted on a major scale, by "non-state actors." It was no longer states as such whose integrity was now threatened, in whose defense they might invoke traditional patriotism: It was the whole structure of international society, on whose effective functioning the well-being of all its members depended. Non-state "terrorists" of a kind had always existed in the shape of domestic rebel groups or extra-national pirates, but their impact had hitherto been marginal and local, posing problems mainly of internal order. Now, in an interdependent world, their activities could have global consequences: With the availability of nuclear weapons, they threatened lethality on a scale comparable to that of a major war. In the United States this new situation has been termed "the war on terror," but even if there is no such all-embracing conflict, there are certainly specific wars being fought in which people are killing and being killed. These deserve to rank as "enlightenment wars," but of a kind rather different from their predecessors.

Hitherto, as we have seen, "enlightenment wars" have been fought by states to preserve or restore peaceful order among themselves. Today they have to be fought, not only against non-state actors, but *on behalf of* non-state actors: that is, of a global, interdependent, *trans*national civil society that transcends states, but on whose effective functioning the entire world depends. In this perspective, 9/11 must be seen not as an act of "war" but as a global "breach of the peace." Its perpetrators, whatever they may think of themselves, should be regarded not as "belligerents" but as transnational criminals against whom it may be necessary to deploy—as in domestic police operations it may be necessary to deploy—limited and strictly controlled armed force in order to preserve the global order that they are seeking to destroy.

For lack of any alternative, such armed force can still be provided only by existing states. States must now be not only the guardians and protectors of their own national interests, but also trustees for the security of that transnational order on which the well-being of their citizens ultimately depends. It is their responsibility as trustees of the global community that now provides a *jus ad bellum* for intervention in regions where events pose an evident danger to that community, giving their armed forces a license to kill and expose themselves to the risk of being killed.

War Must Be Justified in New Ways

The trouble is, the motivation of those forces is still likely to be "Westphalian." That is, they still enlist to fight for their country against its enemies, not act as international policemen on behalf of a global community. They still instinctively think in terms of defeating an enemy and proclaiming a victory, rather than of bringing criminals to justice and maintaining a just order. As Secretary of State Condoleezza Rice once put it, they are not there just to escort kids to school. But if these enlightenment wars are to be fought effectively, it can only be by military forces that possess the restraint and humanity of good policemen who take escorting kids to school as a matter of course and regard killing, though it may occasionally be necessary, as a sign of ultimate failure; a lesson that the forces committed to Iraq have had, rather painfully, to learn.

It is not surprising that states, even the most "enlightened," find this a problem. It still remains easier to motivate young people to fight and die for their "country," antiquated though that appeal may be, than to act as policemen for a "global society"—a concept with which many of them may have little sympathy anyhow—under conditions of great discomfort and danger a very long way from home, where they are confronting adversaries ready and willing both to kill and to die in the name of their own god. To do so demands from the military a new kind of professionalism, at once dispassionate and humane, rather different from the Westphalian readiness to kill and to die in the name of their country against a named and evident enemy.

But we now have to accept that our "countries," however great their power, glorious their pasts and noble their intentions, can no longer be regarded as "Mortall Gods" in whose service it is always legitimate to kill. They can still issue a license to do so, but only in the service of that wider community whose well-being is the ultimate condition of human survival. The reasons we advance to justify our wars, as well as the methods we use to fight them, need to be made relevant to the needs of our own time.

That might provide some comfort for poor Ebenezer.

War and Death Are Acceptable in the Context of American, Christian Beliefs

Kelly Denton-Borhaug

*Kelly Denton-Borhaug is an associate professor of religious stud-
ies at Moravian College in Bethlehem, Pennsylvania.*

*The dominant culture of the United States today is a war
culture, argues Denton-Borhaug in the following viewpoint, and
this war culture is empowered by the rhetoric of sacrifice based
in Christian theology. Denton-Borhaug contends that any discussion concerning soldiers and war centers on the idea that soldiers are making great sacrifices in the name of their country,
and these sacrifices preclude any questioning of the fights in
which they are involved. This vocabulary and the ideas it enables are rooted in the sacrifice Jesus made, giving his life for the
sins of humanity, and its first use can be traced in American history to the Civil War, according to the author. In this first modern, total war, soldiers' deaths and sacrifices were equated to
those of Christ; this, the author suggests, could have been a way
through which people attempted to understand the scale of devastation and loss experienced during this conflict. This trend
continues today, Denton-Borhaug states, and creates a culture in
which war and its associated deaths are accepted and acceptable,
and questions about the nation's war culture are silenced.*

On the eve of the 2008 Democratic Convention in Denver,
Colorado, more than 1,000 antiwar protesters took to the
streets, led by Ron Kovic, the paralyzed Vietnam veteran made
famous by the Hollywood film *Born on the Fourth of July*, and

Kelly Denton-Borhaug, "Sacrifice and U.S. War-Culture," *Prajna Vihara*, vol. 10, no. 1-2,
January/December 2009. Copyright © 2009 by Kelly Denton-Borhaug. All rights reserved. Reproduced by permission.

Cindy Sheehan, mother of Casey Sheehan, a soldier killed in the Iraq war. Carrying signs decrying the use of torture and calling for an end to the war in Iraq, along the way of their march they encountered about 50 counterprotesters. Among them was Nancy Hecker of Colorado Springs, mother of yet another young man killed in Iraq, Major Bill Hecker. "Why are you here for this counterprotest?" she was asked by journalists. Mrs. Hecker replied, "I'm here to honor our son and the sacrifice he made for our country and to support the troops and the families who give so much."

What would we say about the losses associated with war if we did not describe them as sacrifices? Moreover, in a nation still dominantly shaped by Christian religious understandings and practices, how is the same sacrificial language influenced by religious frameworks that emphasize Jesus' sacrificial self-giving life and death? In the United States, language about "the necessity of sacrifice" operates as an electrical conduit between the institutionalization of "war-culture" and the understandings and practices of popular Christianity. At the same time, this conduit is entirely naturalized and mostly unquestioned in U.S. culture at large. As a result, the hinge of sacrifice between nationalism and Christianity remains largely invisible to many if not most U.S. citizens, and the sacred sheen to war-culture contributed by sacrificial language and understandings goes unchallenged. . . .

War-Culture and Christianity Are Central to American Identity

"U.S. war-culture" is the normalized interpenetration of the institutions, ethos and practices of war with ever-increasing facets of daily human life, economy, institutions and imagination in the United States. If "militarism" is a traditional term that refers to the dominance of the military over civilian authority and the prevalence of warlike values in society, contemporary scholars now utilize "militarization" to refer to what I describe as "war-culture." [American anthropology professor at Brown University] Catherine Lutz's definition is particularly apt:

> Militarization is a discursive process, involving a shift in general societal beliefs and values in ways necessary to legitimate the use of force, the organization of large standing armies and their leaders, and the higher taxes or tribute used to pay for them. . . . [It is] an intensification of the labor and resources allocated to military purposes including *the shaping of other institutions in synchrony with military goals* (italics mine).

Lutz's insight regarding the way militarization *shapes* other institutions, perceptions and identities is important here. Militarization does not stand apart as an isolated element in U.S. culture. On the contrary, in the post-9/11 [referring to the September 11, 2001, terrorist attacks] world of the United States, militarization is a powerful force that shapes the dynamics of collective power, life, memory and daily experience. "War-culture" describes how this force has become a driving influence in U.S. culture at large. As Andrew Bacevich [an international relations professor at Boston University] says, "the global military supremacy that the United States presently enjoys—and is bent on perpetuating—has become central to our national identity." . . .

While many scholars and activists have explored and criticized the growth of empire in the post-9/11 United States, less attention has been paid to the significance of the rhetoric and cognitive framework of sacrifice that energizes and enables war-culture and that simultaneously is deeply tied to experiences and practices of Christianity in the U.S. Sacrificial constructions, exactly like the formulation drawn upon by Mrs. Hecker in this [viewpoint's] introduction, are the focus of this investigation. Specifically, I explore the way sacrificial language and frameworks electrically draw together Christianity and war-culture. At the same time, however, not only does the

On September 11, 2001, terrorists attacked the World Trade Center in New York City. This image shows tower number one ablaze after tower number two collapsed. © Frances M. Roberts / Alamy.

cognitive framework of sacrifice act as an internal engine for war-culture, it also provides a sacred canopy over the institutions, culture and practices of war and thus is one important mechanism through which the reality of war-culture is thrust out of conscious view; in other words, not only does the framework of sacrifice energize war-culture, it also plays a decisive role in the normalization of war-culture to the extent that it becomes invisible, and simply part of the expected fabric of life in the U.S. . . .

Sacrificial Rhetoric Dominates Discussions of War

An ROTC [Reserve Officers' Training Corps] student requests that the leaders of the small liberal arts college he attends allow an army Chinook helicopter to land in the central quad of the campus while classes are in session, in order to ferry him to a military training event about seventy miles away. Sound impossible? When this took place at the liberal arts college where I teach in the spring of 2008, I was in the midst of research and writing on this topic. In the immediate aftermath of the helicopter landing, I was fascinated and yet unsurprised to see sacrificial rhetoric emerge almost immediately as controversy regarding the event began to swirl. It all started with a campus-wide email sent by a political science professor on our campus, with just one line: "What is the purpose of this little stunt?" Another professor, this one from the economics and business department, weighed in with another mass email:

> I can think of three worthy purposes, offhand: Those who *sacrifice* salaries and stable home lives, if nothing else, to the service of their country deserve our support. Until the lion lies down peaceably with the lamb, we must encourage young people to consider similar *sacrifices* (italics mine).

In this and further emails from this same professor, sacrificial rhetoric dominated. He wrote about what he viewed as the need to "support those whose sacrifices make our freedoms, including the freedom to wave a peace flag.". . . Moreover, it is just these "sacrifices [that] make the freedom of speech." Such "sacrifice . . . makes freedom possible" and is "required" if we, as a "privileged minority" in the world, wish to continue to enjoy freedom of speech and other freedoms.

The economics professor thus smoothly aligned the presence of the military helicopter on our liberal arts college campus with a portrayal of war as necessary sacrifice. Moreover, his emails argued that the necessity of war as sacrifice is not something to be questioned; in fact, he claimed, its very necessity demands compliance—we are not to question or protest, for that is akin to belittling the central players (soldiers) in this drama. No one challenged the sacrificial theme in this narrative to my knowledge, and even those who disagreed with the same professor relied upon it, such as one student who suggested in his email that making sacrifices (including, he noted, the "ultimate sacrifice") only makes sense when one knows it's going to be "worth it and make a lasting positive impact."

The appearance of sacrificial rhetoric during "Chinook-gate" (as it came to be called by certain members of our campus community) was far from an aberration. In fact, it goes with the territory. Communication scholars have investigated why this is the case, and how such rhetoric operates. Sacrificial rhetoric in the purpose of war-culture has a way of inflating the measurement of real dangers and lifting the specter of peril to a transcendent level. This same overinflation disables critical thinking and pragmatic political critique. The rhetoric of sacrifice is ritualized speech, and channels and legitimates violence by covering the activities of killing with a sacred canopy made up of values such as loyalty and freedom. It "rationalizes war as in the service of the greater glory of God." Robert Ivie [communication and culture professor at Indiana University] writes, "[The] secular quest for security [is converted] into a prayer for redemption and a sacrament of atonement through the sacrifice of a scapegoat in whom we have invested all the evil of the world." Safety becomes the equivalent of salvation in the rhetorical universe that is U.S. war-culture. Moreover, as also is evident from the same economic professor's emails, this rhetoric transforms the idea of "safety" into a feminized, risky and fragile undertaking, a reality that always is "... vulnerable to the rape of the demonic and demented barbarian if left unprotected." Sacrificial rhetoric in the purpose of war-culture enables dehumanization of those considered the enemy, and depersonalizes those other real flesh-and-blood, complicated and multifaceted human beings who all too often are conflated into a one-dimensional portrait, "the troops." Ivie remarks, "In war culture, disembodied abstractions and stone monuments supplant living memories of loved ones sacrificed for country and cause . . . our own soldiers are dehumanized by reducing them to depersonalized heroes."

The Logic of Sacrifice Is Deeply Embedded in U.S. Culture

We in the U.S. have become deeply enculturated to the rhetoric and logic of sacrificialism in war-culture. The predisposition toward sacrificial constructs deeply shapes U.S. citizens' perceptions and equally profoundly impacts our response to the realities of antagonism and conflict. If "the military-industrial-academic (and on and on) complex is a huge systemic behemoth that must be engaged by numerous groups from multiple sites of intervention" [as stated by American cultural critic Henry A. Giroux], it has become all the more important to take on the pedagogical and political challenge to investigate the site of war-culture's intertwined relationship with the rhetoric and cognitive framework of sacrifice. The same relationship electrifies, masks and sacramentalizes war and war-culture and holds at bay pragmatic critique, ethical discernment and the potential to imagine a different reality. War-culture affects everyone who lives in the United States, and many, many more who live in countries outside our borders. Once we become conscious of the deadly links between sacrifice and war-culture, there is no going back. . . .

In modern times, the indelible link between sacrifice and war-culture solidified in the rise of the nation-state. [German American social and cultural historian George L. Mosse stated,] "The modern nation at its birth was a nation in arms." One only need look as far as dominant national symbols, such as the flag, anthems, festivals, memorials, etc., to see that waging war and the rise of the nation-state in modern times are intimately intertwined, to such a degree that it becomes extremely difficult to envision the modern state without war-culture as an essential ingredient in national self-identity and representation. Sacrifice functions as the hinge between war-culture and national self-identity. The wars leading to the birth of the modern state still are explained and justified by making sacred the death of the soldier for the nation, exemplified in national anthems like the "Marseillaise," which proudly proclaims that when its young heroes fall the sacred soil of France will reproduce them all. Likewise, "My country, 'tis of thee / Sweet land of liberty / Of Thee I sing. / Land where my fathers died" are the words of the American anthem learned by every generation of school children. The words of the anthem are paralleled by the famous dictum of Thomas Jefferson, "The tree of liberty must be refreshed from time to time with the blood of patriots and tyrants." Not only a religious artifact, sacrificial self-identity shares an intimate relationship with national identity and representation.

Total War Created a New Context in Which War Must Be Understood

The intensity of this relationship between sacrifice and the nation-state reaches its apotheosis in the development of what scholars term "total war." The difference between this kind of war and earlier wars largely has to do with the entry of new and more extensively deadly forms of technology, and mass participants and victims in war. Total war's targets expand far beyond the enemy soldier. Technological development widens the target focus to include centers of the production of weaponry and also civilian support; as a result, the dead include larger and larger ratios of civilians to each soldier killed (one must also mention in this regard the increasing destruction of the natural world and resulting environmental degradation, accelerating especially in 20th-century war).

The first total war in modern times identified by scholars is the American Civil War, which relied on the mass armies first constructed by Napoleon [Bonaparte] with the added destructive power of new rifled muskets that multiplied target range by five times that of earlier wars. The number of American U.S. soldiers killed in the Civil War amounted to more than in both world wars, plus the Korean and Vietnam wars. In the American Civil War alone, 622,000 soldiers died. Moreover, historians of religion note that it is *precisely* at the point of America's first total war that we discover language entering into American political discourse that compares the sacrifice of the soldier for his country to the sacrifice of Christ. Perhaps, scholars muse, it was the search to find some cognitive framework large enough to encompass such devastating loss in the first U.S. modern total war that led to this specific link. By the end of America's first total war, the Civil War, the Christian sacrificial archetype became fully merged into American civil religion. Both the martyred president and the war dead with whom he was indelibly linked, were understood as those whose sacrificial deaths were ". . . the last full measure of devotion," making possible "a new birth of freedom." The mythic symbolism connecting a cosmic interpretation of Abraham Lincoln's untimely death with the sacrifice of Jesus for salvation entered the nation's bloodstream, as the words from Lincoln's own law partner, [William] Herndon, demonstrated:

> For fifty years God rolled Abraham Lincoln through his fiery furnace. He did it to try Abraham and to purify him for his purpose . . . making him the noblest and loveliest character since Jesus Christ.

Christian proclamation and theological doctrines claiming the sacred sacrifice of Jesus support, justify and provide a model for the sacrifice of the soldier. Both deaths are "necessary" sacrifices in some way, serve a larger social/political or cosmic purpose, provide an ethical blueprint for followers' imitation, and in both cases, the one(s) dying do so as surrogates for others. In the face of losses of many different types, individuals and communities return again and again to sacrificial cognitive frameworks. At the same time, the sacrificial cognitive framework impedes deeper questioning and analysis about the true nature and causes of the losses being experienced. . . .

U.S. Cultural Assumptions About War and Sacrifice Must Be Questioned

U.S. war-culture rests upon a sea bed of cultural assumptions that are reified, naturalized and sacralized by way of religious frameworks. Indeed, the "necessity" of war and the "inevitable" suffering that ensues (and in addition the positioning of such suffering as a "necessary sacrifice" that leads to "salvation"), not to mention the assumed "nobility" associated with the ability to wage war and become formed as a warrior, are cultural givens that the majority of the population assumes to be natural, "just the way things are." Moreover, these assumptions not only are unquestioned, they have achieved a kind of sacred status in contemporary U.S. culture that prevents citizens from more profound examination of the realities of the war-culture in which we live.

War Desensitizes Soldiers to Death and Corrupts Their Morals

Patrick McCormick

Patrick McCormick is a professor of Christian ethics at Gonzaga University in Spokane, Washington.
The US wars in Iraq and Afghanistan have produced a range of morally objectionable acts committed by soldiers and covered by the media. While he maintains that these acts should in no way be condoned, McCormick argues in the following viewpoint that US society should reflect on the conditions of war, soldiers' training, and glorification of war in books and movies that work together to foster an environment in which these war crimes can be committed. He points out that many soldiers who physically survive the battlefield to return to civilian life can still be considered casualties of war due to the traumatic brain injuries or post-traumatic stress disorder from which they suffer, which leave them emotionally scarred and unable to integrate back into society. Further, McCormick blames military training for stripping individuals of their natural tendency not to kill and turning them into individuals who no longer see the enemy as another human, but merely a force that must be annihilated. He concludes that only the war stories that shed light on these negative consequences of war provide an honest assessment of war and the moral sacrifice soldiers must make.

In March the German magazine *Der Spiegel* published photographs of a pair of U.S. soldiers posing with the corpse of an Afghan civilian they are accused of murdering. Stories in the *New York Times* and *Rolling Stone* reported the two sol-

Patrick McCormick, "Morally Wounded," *U.S. Catholic*, vol. 76, no. 6, June 2011. Copyright © 2011 by Claretian Publications. All rights reserved. Reprinted by permission from the June 2011 issue of U.S. Catholic magazine (uscatholic.org).

diers were part of a "kill team" responsible for murdering several innocent Afghans in the first half of 2010, and that members of this group took scores of "trophy" pictures of their dead victims and distributed digital files of this gruesome collection to soldiers in Afghanistan and the United States.

The pose of the two soldiers and the humiliating treatment of their innocent victim's body is reminiscent of pictures from Abu Ghraib. The photographer's intent is to demean and degrade, and the gleeful look on the young soldiers' faces reminds one of photographs from a lynching. The pictures are sickening, and even glancing briefly at them feels obscene and voyeuristic.

Once the military learned of the crimes of the "kill team," 12 low-ranking soldiers were charged and arrested for these atrocities, and every effort was made to confiscate or delete all of the pictures, lest they generate a public outcry and undermine U.S. counterinsurgency strategy in Afghanistan.

The Moral Costs of Combat

There are several disturbing elements to this story. One is that a few young American soldiers committed cold-blooded murder and felt entitled or compelled to take and publish photographs announcing their participation in these war crimes. Another is that a larger group of soldiers copied and collected these gruesome pictures as war mementos. Both of these remind us of the moral costs of combat and suggest that war inflicts more than physical injuries on soldiers.

Alongside the deaths of hundreds of thousands of Iraqis and Afghans and 7,000 U.S. and coalition troops, the wars in Afghanistan and Iraq have produced more than 320,000 traumatic brain injuries, more than 300,000 cases of post-traumatic stress disorder (PTSD), and resulted in a suicide epidemic among soldiers and veterans that has taken more lives than combat. It should not surprise us that these wars have also wounded the souls and character of many soldiers.

American philosopher William James once argued that, for all its horror, war taught our young a set of Spartan virtues they would not learn in civilian life—and this military myth continues in the belief that combat will somehow turn our boys into men. This is certainly the myth of HBO's *Band of Brothers*, Steven Spielberg's *Saving Private Ryan*, and dozens of other war films.

But James and these Hollywood epics overlook the moral injuries inflicted by combat, the psychic wounds that leave so many veterans incapable of returning to normal life.

James looked away from the thousands of shell-shocked, suicidal, and homeless GIs [service members] who make up the long and enduring casualty list of our wars. He closed his eyes to the tragic reality that the horror of war can undo the character of those sent to kill into battle.

Sacrificing the Unwillingness to Kill

Christian ethicist Stanley Hauerwas argues that the greatest sacrifice made in war is the sacrifice of our unwillingness to kill. We do not just ask young men to die for their country, we command them to kill for it.

World War II studies showed that even in combat most American GIs were quite reluctant to kill. Military training was changed to motivate soldiers to kill more readily, but there were psychic and moral costs for this. As psychiatrist Jonathan Shay detailed in *Achilles in Vietnam*, his 1995 study of "combat trauma and the undoing of character," many soldiers are brutalized and injured by the horror of war and the violence they are exposed to and commanded to carry out.

War correspondent Chris Hedges argued in his best-selling book *War Is a Force That Gives Us Meaning* that war is intoxicating and addictive, and that the theater of war creates its own skewed moral universe, a disorienting and polarized world where the enemy is a savage fiend deserving annihilation.

Shay confirms this by describing the way the moral universe of soldiers is reduced to an "us-versus-them" mentality, and how a deadly cocktail of tedium, frustration, terror, and rage at the death of comrades can lead to a berserk state in which murder and atrocities seem acceptable.

The Morality of War Stories

The best war stories ever told have not looked away from the moral injuries inflicted on those asked to make the ultimate sacrifice and kill another human being. Stephen Crane's *Red Badge of Courage* (on the American Civil War), Erich Maria Remarque's *All Quiet on the Western Front* (World War I), and Tim O'Brien's *The Things They Carried* (Vietnam War) take an unblinking look at the horrible things that happen to young men sent into battle. And HBO's more recent *The Pacific* confronts us with the underside of World War II, America's "good war," detailing the way ordinary men are drawn into the savage and murderous maelstrom of combat.

In a similar fashion, the 2007 Iraq war film *In the Valley of Elah* tracks a platoon of young soldiers deeply corrupted by the violence and madness of war, while Kathryn Bigelow's Oscar-winning *The Hurt Locker* uncovers the addictive and intoxicating side of war.

Vietnam vet and author Tim O'Brien has argued that "a true war story is never moral. You can tell a true war story by its absolute and uncompromising allegiance to obscenity and evil." The photographs shot by members of the American "kill team" tell an obscene and evil story. But perhaps other soldiers kept those pictures because the violence resonated with their experience of the madness into which we had sent them.

As long as our official war stories glorify soldiers and combat, we betray those we have commanded to make the ultimate moral sacrifice, pretending we have sent them to war to behave like Boy Scouts.

War Profiteers Still Influence America's Military Spending and Foreign Policy

Kimberly Dvorak

Kimberly Dvorak is a writer living in San Diego, California.

In the following viewpoint, Dvorak criticizes the power of military industrial corporations to influence America's foreign policy. According to Dvorak, leading defense firms spend millions to lobby for contracts and to keep politicians from ending the lucrative war on terror. Dvorak contends that these industries place profits over the lives of soldiers and think nothing of wasting taxpayer money to line their own pockets. Dvorak believes only Congress has the authority to end such waste and bring expensive wars to a close; however, she fears that too many congressional campaigns have been funded by profiteers to make this happen.

As the 2012 presidential race heats up and campaign donations pour into the candidates' war chests, voters should pay attention to the "fog of war" contributors. Last month [in May 2012] President [Barack] Obama signed an executive agreement, at the dismay of most Americans, to remain in Afghanistan for another 10 years. This wartime news labeled the embattled president as a flip-flopper as well as a DC insider. His once "sterling" image of "hope and change" vanished with the swipe of his presidential pen and transformed him into just another "business as usual" presidential incumbent.

Traditionally wartime presidents reap big defense contractor rewards in the form of campaign donations, and by the looks of the pre-election contributions, Obama is poised to be the winner. According to OpenSecrets.org, the defense industry is hedging its bets and lavishing the incumbent president with a two-to-one margin over rival GOP [Republican] presidential wannabe Mitt Romney.

Since 1999 the defense industry has more than doubled its niche in the American manufacturing sector. The industry guru's have deduced that campaign donations of $200 million can produce a return on investment of billions in lucrative Pentagon contracts. The defense lobbying effort certainly pays out high returns and the forecast confirms smooth sailing.

Donating to Presidential Campaigns

So why would President Obama risk his "Nobel Peace" prize and commit more resources to the Middle East? The answer lies with big campaign donors. Obama's new Afghan war 10-year commitment makes a lot more sense after examining his major donors. It turns out that defense contractors are among the president's largest supporters. To be fair, the money usually follows the party in power, but it appears defense contractors are hedging their bets and donating huge sums of money to President Obama's reelection coffers.

As the "President of Peace" enters the final stretch of the expected rough and tumble election, his quick quid pro quo for the new "right" war is being rewarded by the defense industry. For example, power player David Rubenstein, co-founder of the Carlyle Group (one of the largest defense contractors), garners direct access to the White House. According to visitor logs, President Obama hosted Rubenstein on six occasions during his first year in office. Rubenstein also loaned the newly minted president his copy of the Emancipation Proclamation. Obama proudly displays the coveted agreement in the Oval Office.

Could President Eisenhower's warning about the military industrial complex finally become reality? And is the Obama administration banking on support from the largest U.S. defense contractors to pad his reelection coffers ensuring another four years at 1600 Pennsylvania Avenue?

Americans should ask who is benefitting from Obama's "right" war, the soldiers? No. Are the family members of dead and injured soldiers? No. The taxpayers who are covering the billions of dollars per month? No. It appears to be President Obama and the defense industry that is raking in millions of dollars at the expense of service members' lives and limbs.

Dragging Out the War

According to the latest AP [Associated Press] poll only 27 percent of Americans support the Afghanistan war. However, the decade-long war slogs along with no signs of a "winning" strategy or achievable goals.

During a recent *60 Minutes* interview, retired CIA [Central Intelligence Agency] officer Cofer Black who planned and implemented the original Afghanistan covert mission was asked how important are mission plans in Afghanistan? He replied simply, "very."

"The American mission during the early hours after 9/11 (we) sought to destroy al Qaeda and to do so meant removing the Taliban from power," Black explained. Not only was he put in charge of hunting the world's most wanted terrorist, Osama bin Laden, but President George W. Bush tasked the CIA with formulating and launching a war. The classification of war is extremely important, Black explained while he was the CIA counterterrorism center chief. "My mission was not to ensure little girls go to school in Afghanistan. My mission was not to establish a legal system in Afghanistan. My mission was to destroy al Qaeda and to do that we had to overthrow the Taliban."

"We wanted to win," Black vehemently said. He brazenly told President Bush "that when the CIA was finished, there were going to be flies walking across their eyeballs, this isn't a joke, this is a statement of fact of what was going to happen." President Bush didn't flinch.

Black did his job well and engineered a decisive victory with roughly 500 special operation forces that took only a few months to conquer and disband the Talban.

Black attributes the success to the CIA's ability to enter Afghanistan with a lot of cash and their ability to leave a small footprint.

If Mr. Romney wins the 2012 election, inside sources say Cofer Black, former CIA spook, former vice chairman of the largest defense contractor Blackwater USA and current VP [vice president] of Blackbird Technologies, will be his "darkside" go-to guy. In fact, Mr. Romney has already met with and received an intelligence briefing from Cofer Black.

Romney spokesperson Andrea Saul told the Daily Beast that Black is "a well-respected figure in the national security community and said we are pleased to have him on the team." She added that Romney "fields advice from a diverse set of advisers, evaluates their opinions, and ultimately makes his own decisions."

Increasing Wartime Spending

During the 2008 "hope and change" campaign, the junior senator from Illinois admonished the Bush administration, especially VP Dick Cheney, for their misguided and off the books wars. However, once candidate Obama became president the wartime watchdogs were disappointed with Obama's military spending spree. Many continue to be disappointed that war profiteering remains constant under Democratic leadership.

Government watchdogs point out that the $800 billion stimulus package passed in February of 2009 only encouraged more wartime spending. What better way to keep manufacturing plants humming by offering multibillion-dollar Pentagon military no-bid contracts? During Obama's first months in the

White House, the country was shedding jobs at an astounding rate and the new president needed a stopgap measure. The defense industry requires a highly skilled workforce and these jobs accounted for an "increase" in the manufacturing sector, something the Democrats like to champion.

While the stagnant economy remains unpredictable, defense contractors smartly place manufacturing plants in 44 states with influential congressional districts in an effort to flourish off taxpayer money funneled through the Pentagon.

"It's (also) about U.S. alliances, it's about maintaining jobs, and it's about America's broader role in the world—and what you have to do to maintain that role," veteran defense consultant Loren Thompson told CNN news.

Waste and Abuse of Taxpayer Funds

When it comes to reelection contributions, Republicans and Democrats recruit reps across the country to guarantee the Pentagon's billion-dollar contracts. It is the taxpayer that underwrites the large defense contractor manufacturing plants across the country. A prime example of the Chicago-style politics is the Boeing plant located in Obama's backyard. Wily contracting firms strategically placed their plant in a blue-collar state in an effort to buy or to twist the arm of greedy politicians.

While defense contractors reach into at least 44 states to curry political favor they also pay Washington's beltway bandits on K Street a small fortune to cement their interests inside the corporate sector. Many DC lobbyists negotiate billion-dollar contracts using insider information they learned while they were employed at the Pentagon. This is the murky world where defense lobbyists intertwine with the military elite to secure no-bid contracts.

A good example of this revolving door is Army Lieutenant General Robert T. Dail who retired from the service and took an advisory role with LMI, a defense-related business. Many retired military officials move to the private sector defense industry and parlay their inside knowledge to secure billion-dollar contracts. This practice is legal, but many retired officers say it's shameful.

Matt Daigle, of LMI, disagrees with those who are offended by military leaders who go on to work after their service careers end. "Mr. Dail provides our organization with honest and forthright advice regarding the direction and strategy for the company. Furthermore, Mr. Dail served his country with distinction." He continues, "LMI is a not-for-profit government management consultancy. Our support for the federal government extends to more than 40 federal agencies and the military, and is done with transparency and within the rules governing the procurement of services from private businesses. Our work is fairly awarded in accordance with federal acquisition regulations. We do not participate in lobbying, and do not use 'inside information' to secure work that is fairly awarded by our federal clients."

According to a story from CNN, "The money changing hands within the defense industry comes from approximately 85 percent of the Pentagon spending. The industry fat cats have made out since the 9/11 terror attack. The U.S. Defense Department has doubled and spends more in a year than the rest of the world combined. (The U.S. spent $711 billion last year while the rest of the world spent a combined $725)."

"There are a number of legal loopholes that allow the Defense Department, as well as other federal agencies, to avoid competition and to select a single company to provide the desired goods and services. In some cases, there may be only one legitimate supplier of needed goods, or the government can argue that it has 'an unusual and compelling urgency,' and that holding a competition would have a detrimental impact on government operations or national security," an iWatch News story contends.

But those exceptions have become increasingly abused, according to numerous studies. In fact, an analysis of over a dozen government reports and investigations, and interviews with eight former government officials and experts, found a number of concerns about [Department of Defense] competition practices—attributable in large part to the past 10 years of war. Those include:

- The use of large umbrella contracts to purchase goods and services that could be competed individually, thus resulting in lower price;
- Justifying sole source contracts by citing an "urgent and compelling need" when in fact the urgency stemmed from the agency's lack of planning for requirements that have been known for years.
- Extending large contracts as a "bridge" rather than re-competing them.
- An overall failure to utilize competition in cases that could result in cost savings and better performance.

Meanwhile government watchdogs say the enormous spending habits that lead to monumental waste, fraud and abuse show no signs of slowing. A good example of this is the gasoline costs. The American military pays approximately $400 per gallon of fuel to fill up the U.S. convoys inside the landlocked Afghan nation. (The U.S. also pays warlords hush money for safe travels along Afghanistan's insurgent-lined roads.)

"The Special Inspector General for Afghanistan Reconstruction (SIGAR) warned a military commission in January of this year that the entire $11.4 billion for contracts to build nearly 900 facilities for the Afghan National Security Forces is at risk due to inadequate planning. This estimate does not include the waste that has resulted from Afghanistan's inability to sustain projects. Here is an example of pure waste."

Cost-Saving Ideas Rejected

A few years ago a [Pennsylvania] company named Defense Solutions wanted to help the Department of Defense by buying and refurbishing old Soviet Union vehicles and weapons. *New York Times* best-selling author of *Operation Dark Heart*, Army LTC [Lieutenant Colonel] Anthony Shaffer (ret) explained this particular contract was a great idea for three reasons:

First, the Afghan military was already used to using Soviet equipment and vehicles (armored personnel carriers, tanks, helicopters) because they have used the Russian equipment since the Soviet occupation.

Second, the military equipment is low tech, durable, cheap to maintain and easy for the Afghans to use. Common sense dictated that it would be cheaper for NATO [North Atlantic Treaty Organization], Afghanis and the U.S. to pay for the Russian military paraphernalia. However, U.S. corporations sold the Afghans U.S. weapons in an effort to make a lot of money from the Afghans for U.S. technology.

Finally, LTC Shaffer says, "if the Afghan government should fail, we already know how to defeat Soviet/Russian weapon systems—so we would not be providing the Afghans with U.S. weapon systems that are harder to defeat if we had to fight them."

Major U.S. corporations lobbied both the Pentagon and the Hill to push for U.S. weapons to be purchased by the U.S. government and given to the Afghans. "This cost the taxpayers a far greater sum of money than the Russian weapons that could have been purchased from former members of the Warsaw Pact, refurbished and sent to Afghanistan," Shaffer explained. He also said the cost of refurbishing old Soviet gear and giving it to the Afghans would have cost 1/50th of what the U.S. has spent.

It's projected by military commission reports that money lost as a result of the inability to sustain any number of projects could exceed $35 billion in taxpayer money.

As a result, the [Department of Defense] commission proposed adding new positions and authorities to improve coordination and cooperation, including alignment of agency budgets, among defense, state, and USAID [U.S. Agency for International Development] in order to limit waste, fraud and abuse.

So far agencies have failed to set or meet goals for competition in the Middle East wars. In particular, "they have failed and have repeatedly awarded long-term task orders (on a no-compete contract) . . . even when competitive conditions improved; extended contracts and task orders past their specified expiration dates, increased ceilings on cost-type contracts and modified task orders and contracts to add extensive new work; favored using existing task- and delivery-order contracts like LOGCAP III over creating more competitive and more targeted contract vehicles; and used cost-reimbursable contract types even though simpler, fixed-price contracts could expand the competitive pool," the commission concluded.

Poor Prospect of Reform

Moving forward, it's imperative that the Pentagon provides adequate staffing and resources to establish procedures that will protect the taxpayers' interests. It's also up to Congress to stipulate resources for contingency and contracting reforms through legislation that requires regular assessment and reporting of agencies' progress.

Perhaps the most important task Congress is charged with is providing the money used to fund the "unpopular" wars. Ultimately it is the lawmakers that can end the Middle East conflicts with a congressional floor vote; but many of these politicians are guilty of taking defense contractor cash that results in the death and injury to thousands of military service members. Despite having the facts at their fingertips, power and greed inside the beltway continues to justify the means for America's blurry foreign policy.

Soldiers Returning from War Face Post-Traumatic Stress Disorder

Betsy Streisand

Betsy Streisand is a former reporter for U.S. News & World Report. She now is the senior editor for American Public Media's Marketplace.

The trials of combat and the horrific experiences of death have left many US soldiers facing debilitating psychological stress, reports Streisand in the following viewpoint. Dubbed post-traumatic stress disorder (PTSD), this affliction can impair the mental state of frontline troops as well as veterans returning home, Streisand writes. Providing several firsthand accounts from service personnel who have served in the wars in Iraq and Afghanistan, Streisand shows how the disorder can cripple lives and disrupt families. Streisand also explains what treatments are available to veterans and why these services are stretched thin as the numbers of PTSD cases grow.

As they take their seats in the movie theater, Eric and Raquel Schrumpf could be any young couple out on a summer night in Southern California. No one notices as Schrumpf, 31, a former Marine sergeant who served in Iraq, scans the rows for moviegoers who may be wired with explosives under their jackets. No one pays attention as a man who appears to be Middle Eastern, wearing a long coat with bulging pockets, takes a seat in the same row as the Schrumpfs and Eric starts watching him intently. No one listens as Schrumpf instructs his wife to "get as low to the ground as you can if something happens." Then something does. Schrumpf hears metal jangling as the man reaches into his pocket. Convinced he is a suicide bomber about to strike, Schrumpf lunges at him. The man jerks away and his deadly weapon falls to the floor: a can of Coke.

Schrumpf has everyone's attention now, as he and his wife quickly leave the theater. The Schrumpfs can't even remember what movie they went to see. Not that it would have mattered. Eric Schrumpf had room for only one movie in his head, the one where he is in Iraq. Now, more than two years later, Schrumpf has a good job, a strong marriage, a couple of pets, and a life that looks startlingly like everyone else's in Orange County, Calif. But he is still never more than a sound, smell, or thought away from the war. He gets anxious in a crowd, has been known to dive for cover, even indoors, at the sound of a helicopter, reaches for nonexistent weapons to be used in nonexistent circumstances, and wakes up screaming from nightmares about burning bodies and rocket-propelled grenades. "I'll never be the same again," says Schrumpf, who as a weapons and tactics instructor with the 5th Marine Regiment was part of the initial push into southern Iraq in 2003. "The war will be part of my life and my family's life forever."

Reliving the War

Like thousands of soldiers who have returned from Iraq and Afghanistan, Schrumpf is suffering from post-traumatic stress disorder [PTSD], a chronic condition whose symptoms include rage, depression, flashbacks, emotional numbness, and hypervigilance. It can be brought on by a single event, such as when a grenade landed next to Schrumpf, ticking off his death and then failing to explode. Or it can be the result of repeated exposure to trauma such as house-to-house firefights or the accidental killing of civilians. "Soldiers who are routinely exposed to the trauma of killing, maiming, and dying are much more likely to bring those problems home," says Army Col.

Kathy Platoni, a clinical psychologist and leader of a combat stress-control unit that works with soldiers on the battlefield. At its most basic, PTSD is the inability to flip the switch from combat soldier to everyday citizen and to stop reliving the war at so high a frequency that it interferes with the ability to function.

The problem is as old as war itself. But this time, American soldiers have been assured by the government and the military that the solution will be different: Iraq will be nothing like Vietnam, with its legacy of psychologically scarred veterans whose problems went unrecognized, undiagnosed, and untreated. "The hallmark of this war is going to be psychological injury," says Stephen Robinson, a Gulf War vet and director of government relations for Veterans for America in Washington, D.C. "We have learned the lessons of Vietnam, but now they have to be implemented."

Since the war began, the Departments of Defense and Veterans Affairs have stepped up efforts to address the mental health needs of soldiers before, during, and after they are deployed. And more effective treatments for PTSD have been developed. But as the war drags on, the psychological costs are mounting and so is the tab for mental health care. Troop shortages are driving already traumatized soldiers back into combat for three and sometimes four tours of duty. Those who make it home often feel too stigmatized to ask for treatment lest they jeopardize their military careers. And if they do ask, they often can't get the care they need when they need it.

Challenges Faced on the Home Front

In addition, there are concerns among veterans groups that the [George W.] Bush administration is trying to reduce the runaway cost of the war by holding down the number of PTSD cases diagnosed (and benefits paid), and that the promise to protect the mental health of nearly 1.5 million troops is not being kept. "Throughout this war, everything has been

Soldiers from the 3rd Brigade, 1st Cavalry Division, the last US troop brigade to depart Iraq after eight years of war there, celebrate after boarding a C-17 transport plane on December 17, 2011. All US troops departed Iraq by December 31, 2011. Many soldiers who returned home from Iraq will exhibit signs of post-traumatic stress disorder resulting from the horrors they witnessed in the war. © Mario Tama/Getty Images Europe/Getty Images.

underestimated—the insurgency, the body armor, the cost, and the number of troops," says Paul Rieckhoff, an Iraq war vet and founder of Iraq and Afghanistan Veterans of America in New York. "Now, the psychological problems and the needs of these soldiers are being underestimated, too."

Just how many troops will bring the war home with them is impossible to know at this point. But the numbers could be substantial. In a study published in 2004 in the *New England Journal of Medicine*, researchers at the Walter Reed Army Institute of Research found that nearly 17 percent of soldiers who have returned from Iraq, or nearly 1 in 6, showed signs of major depression, generalized anxiety, or PTSD. A report in the *Journal of the American Medical Association* earlier this year [2006] found that 1 in 5 soldiers met the risk for concern. And those numbers are virtually certain to grow as the war enters its fourth year. "I do think we're going to see a whole lot more PTSD as time goes on," says Platoni.

The VA [Department of Veterans Affairs], short of doctors, therapists, and staff in some areas, is straining to meet the mental health needs of the troops who have already returned from Iraq and Afghanistan. Soldiers often wait weeks or even months to see a psychiatrist or psychologist. A 2004 study by the Government Accountability Office found that six of the seven VA medical facilities it visited "may not be able to meet" increased demand for PTSD. "I don't think anybody can say with certainty whether we are prepared to meet the problem because we don't know what the scope is yet," says Matthew Friedman, a psychiatrist and executive director of the VA's National Center for PTSD in White River Junction, Vt. "What we do know is that the greater the exposure to trauma, the greater the chance that someone will have PTSD."

A War Designed to Produce Combat Stress

There may be no war better designed to produce combat stress and trauma. Operation Iraqi Freedom is a round-the-clock, unrelenting danger zone. There are no front lines, it's impossible to identify the enemy, and everything from a paper bag to a baby carriage is a potential bomb. Soldiers are targets 24-7, whether they are running combat missions or asleep in their bunks. "There is no moment of safety in Iraq," says Andrew Pomerantz, a psychiatrist and chief of the Mental Health and Behavioral Science Services at the VA Medical Center in White River Junction. "That's one of the things we're seeing in people when they come back—a feeling of an absolute lack of safety wherever they are."

Stories of vets who sleep with guns and knives and patrol the perimeters of their homes obsessively are as common as tales of valor. Marine Lt. Col. Michael Zacchea, 38, who trained Iraqi troops and was in about 100 firefights, knows that paranoia all too well. "Every time I get on the road," says Zacchea, who commutes from Long Island to Wall Street, "it's like I'm back in the streets of Baghdad in combat, driving and running gun battles, with people throwing grenades at me." Zacchea, a reservist, is now being treated for PTSD at a VA hospital, but had it not been for chronic dysentery, migraines, and shrapnel wounds in his shoulder, he says he probably would have been redeployed in September, emotional scars and all.

And he still may be. The military's need to maintain troop strength in the face of historic recruiting lows means many service members, including some suffering from psychological problems like Zacchea, have no choice but to return. President Bush recently [in August 2006] authorized the Marine Corps to call up inactive reservists, men and women who have already fulfilled their active-duty commitment. "They're having to go deep into the bench," says Robinson, "and deploy some people who shouldn't be deployed."

Unfit for Duty

Robinson is referring to the increasing number of reports of service members who stock antidepressants and sleeping pills alongside their shampoo, soap, and razor blades. The Defense Department [DOD] does not track the number of soldiers on mental health medications or diagnosed with mental illnesses. But the military acknowledges that service members on medication who may be suffering from combat-induced psychological problems are being kept in combat. "We're not keeping people over there on heavy-duty drugs," says Army Surgeon General Kevin Kiley, who estimates that 4 to 5 percent of soldiers are taking medications, mostly sleeping pills. "Four to five percent of 150,000, that's still a lot of troops. But if it's got them handling things, I'm OK with that."

Handling things is a relative term. Army Pvt. Jason Sedotal, 21, a military policeman from Pierre Part, La., had been in Iraq six weeks in 2004 when he drove a Humvee over a land mine. His sergeant, seated beside him, lost two legs and an arm in the explosion. Consumed by guilt and fear, Sedotal, who suffered only minor injuries, was diagnosed with PTSD when he returned from his first tour in early 2005 and given antidepressants and sleeping pills. Several months later, while stationed at Fort Polk, La., he sought more mental health care and was prescribed a different antidepressant.

Last November, Sedotal was redeployed. "They told me I had to go back because my problem wasn't serious enough," Sedotal said in an interview from Baghdad in mid-September. Sedotal says he started "seeing things and having flashbacks." Twice a combat stress unit referred him to a hospital for mental health care. Twice he was returned to his unit, each time with more medication and the second time without his weapon. "I stopped running missions, and I was shunned by my immediate chain of command and my unit," says Sedotal, who returned to Fort Polk last week. . . .

Sending military members who suffer from PTSD back into combat goes straight to one of the toughest issues of the war: how to protect soldiers' mental health and still keep them fighting. It is well established that repeated and prolonged exposure to combat stress is the single greatest risk factor in developing PTSD.

At the same time, there is tremendous resistance to sending home soldiers who are suffering from psychological wounds, in all but the most severe cases. "If a soldier has some PTSD symptoms," says Kiley, "we'll watch him and see how he does." The expectation "is that we're all in this boat together and we need to drive on to complete the mission," he says, adding that if the situation gets worse, the soldier would most likely be given a couple days of rest to see if he recovers. Once soldiers are evacuated, "they are much less likely to come back."

Treatment Programs That Start Early

With that in mind, the DOD has designed a program to manage combat stress and identify mental health problems when they occur. It will include so-called battle-mind training for recruits, which focuses on the emotional fallout of seeing and contributing to the carnage of war and how to deal with it. Once they are in Iraq, there are psychologists and combat stress–control teams, such as Platoni's, who work side by side with troops to help them deal with their emotions and decompress immediately after battle. "Soldiers suffering from combat stress do better if they are treated early, efficiently, and as close to the battlefield as possible," says Col. Charles Hoge, chief of the Department of Psychiatry and Behavioral Sciences at Walter Reed Army Institute of Research.

Currently, there are more than 200 psychiatrists, therapists, social workers, and other mental health experts working with soldiers "in theater." They lend an ear, encourage soldiers to talk about their experiences with each other, and administer whatever short-term remedies they can, including stress-reduction techniques, anger-management strategies, or medications. However, their mission, first and foremost, is to be "force multipliers" who maintain troop strength. Their success is judged by their ability to keep soldiers from going home for psychological reasons. Soldiers are often their allies in this effort, as they feel such guilt and shame over abandoning their units they'll most likely say anything to keep from leaving. "It's a very sticky wicket," says Platoni. "We don't know if our interventions are enough to help them stay mentally healthy, or if they'll suffer more in the long term."

Last year, for instance, Platoni spent four months in Ramadi, near Baghdad, where her battalion was under constant attack by insurgents. "They were watching their fellow soldiers burning to death and thinking they might be next," says Platoni. When a break came, one platoon was removed from combat for 48 hours so they could rest, shower, have a hot meal, and talk to psychologists about what they'd been through. "When they returned to the fighting," says Platoni, "they were able to deal with their fears better and focus on what needed to be done."

When soldiers do return home, the true emotional trauma of war is often just beginning. They go through a cursory post-deployment medical screening and a quick interview with a health care worker, who may or may not specialize in mental health. And returning soldiers are far more likely to downplay emotional problems for fear of being shifted from the "go home" line into the "further evaluation" line and being prevented from seeing families and friends.

Soldiers Do Not Want to Be Stigmatized by PTSD

Three to six months after they return—the time when PTSD symptoms are the most likely to start becoming obvious— troops are given another mental health screening and may be referred for further evaluation, although the chances are slim. A GAO [Government Accountability Office] report issued in May, for instance, found that of the 5 percent of returning veterans between 2001 and 2004 who tested as being at risk for PTSD, fewer than one-quarter were referred for further mental health evaluations. William Winkenwerder, assistant secretary of defense for health affairs, took issue with the study: "We're doing more than any military in history to iden- tify, prevent, and treat mental health concerns among our troops. It is a top priority for us." Even with a referral, many veterans and active-duty soldiers will not seek help for fear of being stigmatized. To help break down the barriers, the DOD has begun encouraging high-ranking soldiers to openly dis- cuss the effects that combat and killing can have on a person's psyche. Even so, the military remains dominated by the image of the macho warrior who sucks it up and drives on. Accord- ing to the VA, the number of PTSD cases has doubled since 2000, to an all-time high of 260,000, but fewer than 40 per- cent of veterans from Iraq and Afghanistan have sought medi- cal treatment. "This is the military culture," says Schrumpf, who now gets regular therapy and takes medication to help with his PTSD. "If it gets out that you even went to see the medical officer, and it always does, then you're done as a career marine. ". . .

New Treatment Approaches

In the past few years, in part because of events such as September 11 [referring to the September 11, 2001, terrorist attacks on the United States], there have been advances in therapies for PTSD. "Just because you have PTSD, it doesn't mean you can't be successful in daily life," says Harold Wain, chief of the psychiatry consultation and liaison service at Walter Reed Army Medical Center in Washington, D.C., the main Army hospital for amputees. Many of the patients Wain sees have suffered catastrophic injuries and must heal their bodies as well as their minds.

Reimagining the trauma again and again, or what's known as exposure therapy, has long been believed to be the most effective way of conquering PTSD. It is still popular and has been made even more effective by such tools as virtual reality. However, therapists are increasingly relying on cognitive behavior therapy or cognitive reframing, putting a new frame around a thought to shift the way a soldier interprets an event. A soldier who is racked with guilt because he couldn't save an injured buddy, for instance, may be redirected to concentrate on what he did do to help. Other approaches such as eye movement desensitization and reprocessing use hypnosis to help soldiers.

For some soldiers, simply talking about what happened to them can be therapy enough. When Zachary Scott-Singley returned from Iraq in 2005, he was haunted by the image of a 3-year-old boy who had been shot and killed accidentally by a fellow soldier. With a son of his own, Scott-Singley couldn't get the picture of the child and his wailing mother out of his head and became increasingly paranoid about his own child's safety. "I was constantly thinking about how people were going to attack me and take him," he says. Scott-Singley twice sought mental health care from the Army. The first time he says he was told that since he wasn't hurting anybody, he didn't have PTSD. The next counselor suggested he buy some stress-management tapes on the Internet and practice counting to 10 whenever he felt overwhelmed. (The VA is legally precluded from discussing a soldier's medical records.) Ironically, Scott-Singley found his therapy on the Web anyway, with his blog *A Soldier's Thoughts* (misoldierthoughts .blogspot.com). "It feels so much better to know I am not alone." . . .

Difficulty Meeting the Demand for Services

The number of veterans from all wars receiving disability payments for PTSD, about 216,000 last year, has grown seven times as fast as the number receiving benefits for disabilities in general, at a cost of $4.6 billion a year. And that figure does not include most of the more than 100,000 Iraq and Afghanistan veterans who have sought mental health services. The IOM [Institute of Medicine] report, released in June, supported the current criteria for diagnosing PTSD.

Now the institute is looking at the accuracy of screening techniques and how to compensate and treat vets with PTSD, widely regarded as an easy condition to fake. And in another move that infuriated veterans groups, the VA late last year proposed a review of 72,000 cases of vets who were receiving full disability benefits for PTSD to look for fraud. The move prompted such an outcry that it was called off.

Studies and reviews aside, there isn't enough help available to veterans with PTSD. According to a report from the VA, individual veterans' visits to PTSD specialists dropped by 20 percent from 1995 to 2005—"a decrease in capacity at a time when the VA needs to reach out," the report stated. Secretary of Veterans Affairs James Nicholson says the VA sees 85 percent of new mental health patients within 30 days. "But that still leaves 15 percent and that's a big number. Could we do better? Yes."

Bush has called for a record $80.6 billion in the 2007 VA budget. That includes $3.2 billion for mental health services, a $339 million increase over this year's budget. However, those increases are being met by increasing demands for care, as well as rising cost-of-living allowances and prescription drug prices. "The bigger budget doesn't really add up to much," says Rieckhoff.

However frustrating and exhausting the process, most vets can avoid getting help only so long before friends and family push them into counseling or they get in trouble with the law. "It's almost like your family has its own form of PTSD just from being around you every day," says a former Army sergeant who worked as an interrogator in Iraq and asked that his name be withheld. "When I came back I was emotionally shut down and severely paranoid. My wife thought I was crazy and my son didn't realize who I was. Because of them, I got help."

Finding Someone to Talk To

Like many soldiers, he found it at one of more than 200 local veterans centers, which offer counseling for PTSD and sexual assault, a growing concern for women in the military. Vet centers are part of the VA but operate like the anti-VA, free of the delays and bureaucracy. There is almost no paperwork, and the wait to see a counselor is rarely more than a week. It's no coincidence that when *Doonesbury* [comic strip] character B.D. finally went for help with his PTSD, he went to a vet center. The centers are small and staffed mostly by vets, which creates the feel of a nurturing social environment rather than an institutional one. The free coffee is strictly decaf, and the approach is laid back. "Someone may come in asking about an insurance problem, and as we answer their questions, we ask them how are they feeling," says Karen Schoenfeld-Smith, a psychologist and team leader at the San Diego vet center, which sees a lot of Iraq vets from nearby Camp Pendleton. "That's how we get them into it." Many come just to talk to other vets.

It is that same need to talk that keeps Schrumpf emailing and phoning fellow Marines and returning to Camp Pendleton every couple of weeks to hang out. "It is the only place I can talk about the killing," he says. Next month, Schrumpf will leave California for his home state of Tennessee, where he says it will be easier to raise a family. He's not worried about taking the war with him. In fact, in many ways he is more worried about leaving it behind. "The anger, the rage, and all that is just there," says Schrumpf. "And honestly, I don't want it to leave. It's like a security blanket." Or a movie, that just keeps on playing.

For Further Discussion

1. Literary critics have been torn on whether to categorize *A Farewell to Arms* as a war story or a romance. How would you classify the novel? Using the viewpoints in this anthology and any other pertinent readings you may have found, explain how you arrived at this interpretation. Be sure to cite what details and what larger themes of the novel influenced your outlook on the story.

2. Lawrence R. Broer contends that while *A Farewell to Arms* depicts the horrors of war, Hemingway's prose still revels in the glories of the battlefield and promotes a very masculine view of heroism and the soldierly life. William Dow, on the other hand, believes Hemingway's "poetic" prose style evokes the haunting tragedy of conflict without exalting its violent nature. After reading these viewpoints and the biographical information in earlier viewpoints, explain how you think Hemingway views warfare, and decide whether *A Farewell to Arms* conveys Hemingway's attitude as you understand it.

3. Some reviewers of *A Farewell to Arms* emphasize the role of religion in shaping Frederic Henry's attitudes about love, life, and death. James F. Light, however, asserts that Frederic dismisses religion as inadequate to contain and explain the emotions and ideals he expresses as the novel progresses. Light maintains that Frederic puts his faith in a personal "religion" that derives from braving death— conquering the fear of mortality by staring it in the face. Do you agree with Light's conclusion? What do you think Frederic comes to believe in by the end of the novel? Give evidence to support your claim.

4. Patrick McCormick claims that the traumas of war condition soldiers to hold life cheaply and relinquish some of their personal convictions concerning right and wrong. Using any news reports or your own experiences with veterans, explain whether you think McCormick is correct in his assessment. Then, consider McCormick's view in light of *A Farewell to Arms*. Do you think Frederic Henry has suffered in the way McCormick describes? Be sure to support your claims with evidence from the work.

5. Kimberly Dvorak argues that war profiteers still influence America's foreign policy and encourage the nation to stay on a war footing to reap the economic benefits. Hemingway also indicted war profiteers, claiming in his preface to the 1949 edition of *A Farewell to Arms* that they were worthy of being shot for their actions. What attitudes do you see expressed in *A Farewell to Arms* concerning the dichotomy between those who run the war and those who fight it? How does this influence your understanding of Hemingway's view of war?

For Further Reading

Stephen Crane, *The Red Badge of Courage*. New York: Penguin, 2009.

John Dos Passos, *Three Soldiers*. Mineola, NY: Dover, 2004.

Sebastian Faulks, *Birdsong: A Novel of Love and War*. New York: Vintage, 1997.

Ernest Hemingway, *By-Line, Ernest Hemingway: Selected Articles and Dispatches of Four Decades*. Ed. William White. New York: Simon & Schuster, 1998.

————, *The Collected Stories*. New York: Everyman's Library, 1995.

————, *Death in the Afternoon*. New York: Simon & Schuster, 1996.

————, *Ernest Hemingway Selected Letters 1917–1961*. Ed. Carlos Baker. New York: Scribner, 2003.

————, *For Whom the Bell Tolls*. New York: Scribner, 1996.

————, *The Sun Also Rises*. New York: Scribner, 1996.

Tim O'Brien, *Going After Cacciato*. New York: Broadway Books, 1999.

Erich Maria Remarque, *All Quiet on the Western Front*. New York: Ballantine, 1982.

Bibliography

Books

Anthony Burgess   *Ernest Hemingway*. New York:
                  Thames and Hudson, 1999.

Daniel Byman   *The Five Front War: The Better Way
                  to Fight Global Jihad*. Hoboken, NJ:
                  John Wiley & Sons, 2008.

Mark Cirino   *Ernest Hemingway: Thought in Action*.
                  Madison: University of Wisconsin
                  Press, 2012.

Dexter Filkins   *The Forever War*. New York: Alfred A.
                  Knopf, 2008.

Ernest   *Hemingway on War*. Ed. Seán
Hemingway   Hemingway. New York: Scribner,
                  2003.

Paul Hendrickson *Hemingway's Boat: Everything He
                  Loved in Life, and Lost, 1934–1961*.
                  New York: Alfred A. Knopf, 2011.

Sebastian Junger *War*. New York: Twelve, 2010.

Jane Mayer   *The Dark Side: The Inside Story of
                  How the War on Terror Turned into a
                  War on American Ideals*. New York:
                  Anchor Books, 2009.

George Packer   *The Assassins' Gate: America in Iraq*.
                  New York: Thorndike Press, 2005.

Rupert Smith

The Utility of Force: The Art of War in the Modern World. New York: Vintage, 2008.

Henry Serrano Villard and James Nagel, eds.

Hemingway in Love and War: The Lost Diary of Agnes von Kurowsky, Her Letters and Correspondence of Ernest Hemingway. Boston, MA: Northeastern University Press, 1989.

Linda Wagner-Martin

Ernest Hemingway: A Literary Life. New York: Palgrave Macmillan, 2007.

Arthur Waldhorn

A Reader's Guide to Ernest Hemingway. Syracuse, NY: Syracuse University Press, 2002.

Periodicals

William Adair

"The Sun Also Rises: The Source of *A Farewell to Arms,"* ANQ, Fall 1999.

Jamie Barlowe

"'They Have Rewritten It All': Film Adaptations of *A Farewell to Arms,"* *Hemingway Review,* Fall 2011.

Stephen Bates

"'An Apostle for His Work': The Death of Lieutenant Edward Michael McKey," *Hemingway Review,* Spring 2010.

Jack Beatty

"Ernest Hemingway and His World," *New Republic,* October 7, 1978.

Jackson J. Benson

"Ernest Hemingway: The Life as Fiction and the Fiction as Life," *American Literature,* October 1989.

Ron Capshaw · "Hemingway: A Static Figure Amidst the Red Decade Shifts," *Partisan Review*, Summer 2002.

Peter W. Chiarelli and Stephen M. Smith · "Learning from Our Modern Wars: The Imperatives of Preparing for a Dangerous Future," *Military Review*, September/October 2007.

Mark Cirino · "'A Bicycle Is a Splendid Thing': Hemingway's Source for Bartolomeo Aymo in *A Farewell to Arms*," *Hemingway Review*, Fall 2006.

Melissa Burdick Harmon · "Ernest Hemingway: The Man and His Demons," *Biography*, May 1998.

Sebastian Junger · "Combat High," *Newsweek*, May 10, 2010.

Sam Kean · "From Soldiers to Veterans, Good Health to Bad," *Science*, June 8, 2012.

James Kurth · "The Soldier, the State, and the Clash of Civilizations: The Legacy of Samuel Huntington," *Orbis*, March 2010.

D.T. Max · "Ernest Hemingway's War Wounds," *New York Times*, July 18, 1999.

Jeffrey Meyers · "Ernest Becoming Hemingway," *Yale Review*, July 2012.

Brian Mockenhaupt · "A History of Violence: How the Army Is Trying to Capture the Lessons of War," *Atlantic Monthly*, April 2011.

Nation	"Time to Get Out of Afghanistan," April 2, 2012.
Margot Norris	"The Novel as War: Lies and Truth in Hemingway's *A Farewell to Arms*," *Modern Fiction Studies*, Winter 1994.
Katie Owens-Murphy	"Hemingway's Pragmatism: Truth, Utility, and Concrete Particulars in *A Farewell to Arms*," *Hemingway Review*, Fall 2009.
John Pekkanen	"Soldiers Take One Step at a Time with Prosthetic Limbs," *Washingtonian*, August 2011.
Aimee L. Pozorski	"Infantry and Infanticide in *A Farewell to Arms*," *Hemingway Review*, Spring 2004.
Dianna Prenatt	"'How to Tell a True War Story': Reading One of Ours Through Sergeant's *Shadow-Shapes* and Hemingway's *A Farewell to Arms*," *Willa Cather Newsletter & Review*, Spring/Summer 2009.
Matthew C. Stewart	"Ernest Hemingway and World War I: Combatting Recent Psychobiographical Reassessments, Restoring the War," *Papers on Language & Literature*, Spring 2000.
Daniel Stone, Eve Conant, John Barry, and Larry Kaplow	"Love Is a Battlefield," *Newsweek*, June 15, 2009.

Brenda Wineapple "The Sun Also Sets," *Nation*, June 14, 1999.

Index